LEADERSHIP QUESTIONS for

Health Care Professionals

Applying Theories & Principles to Practice

LEADERSHIP QUESTIONS for

Health Care Professionals

Applying Theories & Principles to Practice

Matthew R. Kutz, PhD, AT, CSCS
Associate Professor
Bowling Green State University
Athletic Training Program
Senior Associate Editor
Athletic Training Education Journal

SLACK
INCORPORATED

www.Healio.com/books

ISBN: 978-1-63091-361-8

Published by: SLACK Incorporated
                 6900 Grove Road
                 Thorofare, NJ 08086 USA
                 Telephone: 856-848-1000
                 Fax: 856-848-6091
                 www.Healio.com/books

Contact SLACK Incorporated for more information about other books in this field or about the availability of our books from distributors outside the United States.

Library of Congress Cataloging-in-Publication Data

Names: Kutz, Matthew R., author.
Title: Leadership questions for health care professionals : applying theories
  and principles to practice / Matthew R. Kutz.
Description: Thorofare, NJ : Slack Incorporated, [2018] | Includes
  bibliographical references and index.
Identifiers: LCCN 2017057090 (print) | LCCN 2017058128 (ebook) | ISBN
  9781630913625 (e-book) | ISBN 9781630913632 (Web) | ISBN 9781630913618
  (paperback : alk. paper)
Subjects: | MESH: Leadership | Health Personnel | Interprofessional Relations
  | Communication
Classification: LCC RA971 (ebook) | LCC RA971 (print) | NLM W 21 | DDC
  362.1068/4--dc23
LC record available at https://lccn.loc.gov/2017057090

Printed in the United States of America.

Last digit is print number: 10   9   8   7   6   5   4   3   2   1

Dedication

This book is dedicated to my athletic training students who have forced me to "get to the point" when answering leadership questions. Their insistence on brevity and relevance has forced me to refine and develop many of these insights.

Contents

Acknowledgments

No book, no matter how personal or well-developed, is the product of a single person's thought or effort. I wish to thank the thousands of participants in my lectures, workshops, and seminars who have inspired many of these questions. I wish to thank my good friend and colleague Dr. Debra Ball who was instrumental in helping me develop a meaningful and relevant list of leadership questions. Many of the questions and issues we have discussed in personal conversations ended up here in this volume. Thank you Deb! Finally, I must thank the love of my life and best friend, Angie, for her support and encouragement. Honey, you rock!

About the Author

Matthew R. Kutz, PhD, AT, CSCS is an Associate Professor of Exercise Science and Sports Medicine in the College of Education and Human Development at Bowling Green State University, a 2013 Fulbright Scholar in the Medical Sciences (University of Rwanda, College of Medicine and Health Science [formerly Kigali Health Institute]), and a 2016 Visiting Research Fellow and Visiting Scholar at Gold Coast University Hospital and Griffith University, College of Medicine, Health Service Management (Queensland, Australia). Matt is a Senior Associate Editor of the *Athletic Training Education Journal*, a member of the National Athletics Trainers' Association International Committee, and a member of the Commission on Accreditation of Athletic Training Education Ethics and Professional Standards Committee. In addition to his international and professional service, Matt is the award-winning author of *Contextual Intelligence: How Thinking in 3D Can Help Resolve Complexity, Uncertainty, and Ambiguity* (Palgrave MacMillan) and *Leadership and Management in Athletic Training: An Integrated Approach* (Jones and Bartlett).

Preface

This book is all about you. It was written to help you become a better leader. Medicine and health care are already difficult to navigate, and not being aware of some of the common leadership questions can be a disadvantage. The intention of this book is to facilitate intrigue and dialogue about the general concept of leadership and to give you a broader perspective relative to leadership issues. If you are already asking these questions, then hopefully the responses will give you an opportunity to critically reflect on how you can answer them for your situation.

I am convinced that one of the best ways to learn about leadership is to ask questions and hear other perspectives. I hope my responses offer another perspective. Please note, that I am offering responses to these questions and not "answers," per se. While these are *my* answers, they are not *the* answers. They are merely my thoughtful responses based on my 2 decades of working with leaders and the scholarly literature.

By asking questions that many leaders have asked at various stages of their leadership journey, it is my hope to help you along your leadership journey. I must tell you this is not an entry-level book. Yes, it is for novice leaders and aspiring leaders, but you may have 10 or even 20 years of experience as a clinician, professional, or administrator, and still may need to hear and think about these responses for your own practice. It is my hope that the discussion questions posed at the end of each response require you to engage in critical thinking and re-evaluate your experiences in order to find new insights.

I do not believe you can just wake up one morning and decide, "Today is the day I am going to *be* a leader." You may decide on *becoming* a leader, even if you have been a manager or supervisor for some time, but becoming is an intentional process that often starts with asking and answering questions like the ones I have posed here. This is not a book that will give you the answers on how to be a great leader, but it is a book that asks questions that will hopefully spur on and foster additional questions that you work to answer during your leadership development process.

When first developing this book, I had come up with over 100 questions related to leadership. After consultation and refining the list, I was able to cull it down to the top 30 or so. Hopefully these are practical enough to help you process leadership within your specific health care domain. This book is not intended for one specific profession, but was written to help everyone within health care. Whether you are a nurse, medical doctor, athletic trainer, physical therapist, occupational therapist, speech-language pathologist, medical technician, or health care administrator—these questions are relevant.

This text is best used as a supplement and critical thinking guide to administration and leadership courses. The questions are organized into different sections. Section I consists of questions about the essence of leadership. For example, it discusses what leadership is, how it is defined, and how it is different from management. Section II consists of questions about leadership development. For example, leadership can be learned and how it is learned. Section III consists of questions about teamwork and communication. Section IV asks questions about change. Section V asks about organizational culture and complexity. Section VI consists of questions about ethics and power. Finally, Section VII asks questions about international and multicultural leadership. Each section consists of several questions, and following each question are discussion questions designed to facilitate class or group dialogue. Have fun exploring leadership, and I hope this text fosters more leadership questions for you.

Introduction

Leadership has been the joy of my life and the bane of my existence. In fact, when I think of my leadership journey, it reminds me of Charles Dickens' iconic opening lines from *A Tale of Two Cities*: "It was the best of times, it was the worst of times, it was the age of wisdom, it was the age of foolishness, it was the epoch of belief, it was the epoch of incredulity."[1] Many of us have had a love-hate relationship with leadership. At the very least, we can all think of leaders in our past who we have loved and who we have loathed. Perhaps that is true of the same leader on different days. This reality makes leadership a very tumultuous and ambiguous phenomenon. As such, it can bring great joy and great frustration. This is true in terms of our own leadership and followership. At times, we practice leadership well, and other times demonstrate it with extremely poor dexterity. Likewise, at other times our leaders lead in ways that inspire us, and the next day disappoint us. Regardless, leadership is critical to understand and even more so in contexts like health care that are under siege and always changing. Few other industries are as volatile, uncertain, complex, and ambiguous—or as some say, VUCA—as health care. Consequently, leadership is in high demand and understanding what it is and how it works is a valuable commodity. Health care clinicians and administrators who engage in high-level leadership behaviors are poised to make the most significant and meaningful contributions to the future of health care. Not only in terms of improved patient outcomes, higher quality care, and interprofessional practice, but in future-making.

Sir Charles Geoffrey Vickers, winner of the Victoria Cross, lawyer, renowned systems scientist, and author of numerous books, is sometimes credited for saying, "My message is…what my experience has fitted me to see and say."[2] I too, would like to echo that sentiment. My experience is from where I drew much of this manuscript. Using evidence-based language, it is the scholarship of practice that I rely on primarily for the template of this book. Knowing that an essential aspect of evidence-based practice (EBP) is the clinician's experience, I have endeavored to stay true to that. The trinity of EBP is best available clinical evidence, clinician's experience, and patient's expectations. Well, you are the patients in this case, and I have raised questions that should be of particular interest to you. My experience, combined with peer-reviewed scholarship (from the leadership and organizational behavior domains), are also leveraged heavily. Therefore, one might conclude this is an evidence-based approach (although loosely defined).

Practicing leadership in various roles throughout my career has been extremely rewarding, but not without grief. I have learned a lot about people and organizations, but even more about myself. Leadership will do that, if you let it. It will teach you about yourself.

The process of leadership is not easy, but it has the capacity to make one better. It is this hope that inspires me to write this book for you. For over 2 decades, I have been a practicing health care professional (athletic trainer), and in that time I have served in numerous leadership capacities. I have been a program director and clinical coordinator. I have chaired committees, served as district representative to my state association, worked on numerous teams, led study abroad courses, and held many other professional roles and responsibilities. My life outside of my professional work has been rich with opportunities to lead as well. Not only as a father and collaborative partner with my wife leading our household, but also by serving on civic and religious organizations in various leadership capacities. Not only have I been a leadership scholar and researcher, but also an organizational consultant with for-profit and nonprofit groups, ranging from small organizations to Fortune 500 multinational, global corporations. All of these have been rewarding experiences, and, as I've already alluded to, required hard work and some painful (and embarrassing) lessons; some I am sure I will have to relearn. Becoming a leader is real work. Start with practicing leadership behaviors with more frequency, ask yourself the questions identified in this book, and be purposeful about responding honestly to the discussion questions. Enjoy your journey.

References

1. Dickens, C. *A Tale of Two Cities*. London, United Kingdom: Chapman & Hall; 1874.
2. Vickers, J. *Rethinking the Future: The Correspondence Between Geoffrey Vickers and Adolph Lowe*. New Brunswick, NJ: Transaction Publishers; 1991.

SECTION I

QUESTIONS ABOUT THE ESSENCE OF LEADERSHIP

QUESTION 1

Why Does Everyone Make Such a Big Deal Out of Leadership?

The Importance of Leadership

Few other concepts have captured the imagination of people like leadership. One of the fascinating realities about leadership is that people have been discussing and writing about it for millennia. One of the earliest recorded complete works on leadership is an Egyptian papyrus dated between 3580 and 3536 BC, and consists of instructions of Ptah-Hotep, an ancient Egyptian vizier, to his son on how to govern a city. With a history like that, few people endeavor to question leadership's importance. In fact, leadership guru John Maxwell is credited with one of the most often quoted leadership axioms ever, "everything rises and falls on leadership."[1] The obvious implications of a statement like that is that leadership is important. That is not to say there is no debate about how important leadership is, relative to the myriad of other factors that contribute to organizational success, but only that it is important. To demonstrate, consider that American companies spend almost $14 billion annually on leadership development.[2] By that standard alone, never mind any empirical outcomes, someone somewhere thinks leadership is important enough to continue to invest in it. Using the metric of investment dollars alone we could answer our question matter-of-factly.

For some people, leadership is a mythical superpower, and to others it is a clearly delineated list of competencies or capabilities. Some scholars and practitioners believe it is person-centric or trait-based and others hold to the notion that it is a process. For sure, there is significant debate on what leadership is and how one becomes a leader. However, despite the ontology (the nature of being) concerning leadership, there is virtually no viable argument that leadership is not important at all. With that said, it is necessary to explicitly state, based on consensus, that leadership is important. Using the metrics of investment dollars and expert consensus we see that leadership is important. However, on the off-chance that everybody is wrong, and therefore wasting their money, let us look briefly at some empirical evidence related to outcomes and the necessity of leadership within professional practice.

Kutz MR. *Leadership Questions for Health Care Professionals:*
Applying Theories & Principles to Practice (pp 3-18).
© 2018 SLACK Incorporated.

Within the context of health care, it has been reported to be significantly important. For example, peer-reviewed literature in nursing, athletic training, medicine, and physical therapy all report the benefits and necessity of leadership to clinical practice and the advancement of professions. In addition to these, there is a plethora of evidence from industrial psychologists, business managers, and organizational theorists that we will not review, that advocates for leadership's importance in personal and organizational success. For a few quick examples, let's look at several different health care profession's literature about leadership behaviors.

The Board of Certification (the organization that conducts and dispenses the Role Delineation Study and Practice Analysis for Athletic Trainers) has said that athletic trainers "must utilize leadership techniques to compete in today's health care market."[3] The presumption of course is that leadership is necessary to stay sustainable and compete in a volatile and uncertain health care industry. The Institutes of Medicine (IOM), suggests that the nursing profession must produce leaders at every level of the system.[4] This recommendation is based on the complexity in which health care is practiced, requiring leadership throughout a health care organization and not just at the higher organizational levels. Among physical therapists, it has been stated that physical therapists at all levels will need to take on leadership responsibilities, and thus, will require leadership training.[5] This recommendation is also based on the volatility and uncertainty within health care, which requires leadership at every level. And finally, the 1998 Pew Health Commission[6] has recommended that all health care workers intending to practice in the 21st century, whether they seek management positions or not, should learn leadership behaviors. Note the Pew Health Commission's recommendation that leadership is something to be practiced, irrespective of a management position. Interestingly enough, we are already beginning to see leadership being represented as distinct from management. Therefore, we can add that leadership is important even if one is not a formal leader, per se. Furthermore, all these recommendations are based on evidence that leadership leads to positive organizational outcomes, and more importantly, leads to improved clinical outcomes. Not only has leadership contributed to higher patient satisfaction and fewer errors,[7] but some preliminary research also seems to indicate that clinical skills seem to be improved when leadership is practiced by clinicians.[8] Finally, the IOM states that the clinical education community needs to "provide transformational leadership in response to the challenges" that are threatening health care today.[9] Without transformational leadership being embedded into curriculum and practiced clinically, the health care industry may not be able to handle the challenges it faces. Is leadership important? Yes. Should leadership be taught and measured in professional education programs? Yes.

Discussion Questions

1. What are some reasons that you believe leadership is (or is not) important?
2. How can the importance of leadership be measured in health care?
3. Is leadership more (or less) important in health care vs other venues such as government or business?
4. Is leadership a "superpower" for some, but not all? Or is it something everyone can do?

References

1. Maxwell JC. *The 21 Indispensable Qualities of a Leader: Becoming the Person Others Will Want to Follow*. Nashville, TN: Thomas Nelson; 1999.
2. Loew L, O'Leonard K. Leadership development factbook 2012: benchmarks and trends in U.S. leadership development. Bersin Web site. http://www.bersin.com/Practice/Detail.aspx?docid=15587&mode=search&p=Leadership-Development. Published July 16, 2012. Accessed July 26, 2017.
3. Board of Certification, Inc. *Role delineation study and Practice Act*. Omaha, NE: Board of Certification, Inc; 2011.
4. Porter-O'Grady T. Leadership at all levels. *Nurs Manage*. 2011;42(5):32-37.
5. McGowan E, Stokes EK. Leadership in the profession of physical therapy. *Phys Ther Rev*. 2015;20(2):122-131.
6. Pew Health Professions Commission. *Twenty-one competencies for the twenty-first century*. San Francisco, CA: UCSF Center for the Health Professions; 1998.
7. Wong CA, Cummings GG. The relationship between nursing leadership and patient outcomes: a systematic review. *J Nurs Manage*. 2007;15(5):508-521.
8. Kutz MR. Leadership is positively related to athletic training students' clinical behaviors. *Athl Train Educ J*. 2012;7(3):95-102.
9. Institute of Medicine. *Health Professions Education: A Bridge to Quality*. Washington, DC: The National Academies Press; 2003.

QUESTION 2

So, if Leadership Is so Important, What Is It Exactly?

What Is Leadership?

Based on the assumption that leadership is important, it is impossible to go any further until we answer the foundational question of, "What is leadership?" The problem in answering that question succinctly is that there is no single agreed upon definition of what leadership is. There are so many different definitions of leadership, and so many nuances to how and when it is applied, that it is nearly impossible to sort through them all. In fact, it is likely that you will have as many definitions of leadership as there are people to define it. Therefore, this may be one of the most significant leadership question anyone will ever answer. If, for no other reason, the answer establishes an individual's or organization's philosophical leadership assumptions. Indeed, answering the question, "What is leadership?" is a prerequisite to it occurring at all. Without an agreed-upon definition, it is impossible to evaluate if it is happening at all. To do that, it is necessary to look to the literature.

While there are virtually thousands of definitions of leadership, there are enough "common threads" between definitions that a reasonable idea of how leadership can be defined can be formulated. Perhaps one of the most common definitions of leadership, and one that is attributed to many different authors, is that it is "influence." Rankin and Ingersoll[1] define leadership as "the ability to influence others toward the achievement of goals." Ray[2] describes it as "the process of influencing the behavior and attitudes of others to achieve intended outcomes." Others within health care define leadership as "the ability to facilitate and influence superiors, peers, and subordinates to make recognizable strides toward shared or unshared objectives."[3] Yet, others describe leadership as "an influence relationship among leaders and followers who intend real changes that reflect their mutual purposes."[4] There are more who define leadership as "successful and sustainable change, holds multiple lenses and perspectives, strengthens and builds relationships, inspires and engages others to grow, leads across complex systems, asks questions and reflects on and senses what is needed most in a system."[5]

When analyzing these definitions and descriptions, it is clear that leadership includes at least 3 elements:

1. Influence
2. Measurable results
3. Interaction

Influence is explicitly expressed in each of the previous definitions, and at least implicitly impli in most others. Influence has been defined as the "ability to affect the behavior of others,"[3] which is further described as a force that transcends organizational hierarchy or job titles. In other words, influence is not dependent on a person's title or whether he or she has formal authority. Other health care literature supports the notion that leadership is based on influence that transcends a job description, title, or role.[6] So, based on these descriptions we can say that leadership is being able to affect people's behavior toward achieving something. Whether that something is agreed upon by all parties involved is also subject to debate. Regardless, measurable results implies forward movement of some kind. Leadership is about getting people to places they have never been to or can't get to on their own. This leads us to the third element of what leadership is, and that is interactive. Leadership cannot be demonstrated in isolation. It must necessarily include an interaction of some kind between people. Taking these 3 elements into account we can, rather simply, say that leadership is the ability to influence people to achieve something that they have not previously accomplished.

Discussion Questions

1. How do you define leadership?
2. Has your definition or understanding of leadership changed?
3. How can you, as a health care provider, wield more influence over people without coercion or manipulation?
4. What aspects of leadership success are measurable in health care?
5. Given the 3 elements of leadership mentioned in the chapter, do you or your organizations measure leadership accurately?

References

1. Rankin JM, Ingersoll CD. *Athletic training management: Concepts and applications.* McGraw-Hill Companies; 2005.
2. Ray R. *Management strategies in athletic training.* Human Kinetics Publishers; 2005.
3. Kutz MR. *Leadership and management in athletic training: An integrated approach.* Lippincott Williams & Wilkins; 2010.
4. Nellis SM. Leadership and management: techniques and principles for athletic training. *J Athl Train.* 1994;29(4):328.
5. Canadian Physiotherapy Association Leadership Division. Framework for professional development of leadership core competencies: Canadian Physiotherapy Association. Canadian Physiotherapy Association Web site. http://www.physiotherapy.ca/getmedia/62c59938-be84-4062-bcc8-939145698b98/CPA-Leadership-Education-Report-FINAL.pdf.aspx. Published 2012. Accessed July 26,2017.
6. Byram DA. Leadership: a skill, not a role. *AACN Clin Issues.* 2000;11(3):463-469.

I Learned A Lot of Management in College—Is That the Same as Leadership?

The distinction between leadership and management (and leaders and managers) can be a slippery slope to navigate. While there certainly are similarities, and the consensus is certainly not unanimous, much of the scholarly literature seems to lean toward the 2 being considered separate constructs.[1] This does not mean that leaders and managers want different outcomes or are trying to achieve something different from the other—in fact, both usually want similar outcomes, like fewer medical errors, increased revenue, higher efficiency, or greater patient satisfaction. To complicate matters further, it is not uncommon for a single person to demonstrate both leadership and management behaviors. There is definitely overlap between management and leadership, but there is also a great deal that differentiates them.

Leadership and management skills are complementary, but their origins and philosophical foundations are different.[2] Understanding these differences is absolutely essential if effective leadership development programs are to be crafted and leadership performance evaluated fairly.[3] Management aims to maintain standardization, consistency and order, and it is concerned with the efficient and effective running of organizations. Leadership aims to create change and improvement.[4]

Harvard organizational psychologist, Abraham Zaleznik[5] argued that the difference between managers and leaders is based in the unconscious conceptions they hold about chaos and order. He claimed that managers tend to prefer procedure, seek stability and control, and instinctively handle problems before they fully understand their significance. In contrast, he believed that leaders are much better at tolerating chaos and the absence of obvious structure, and are often more willing to delay closure in order to understand problems more accurately. These differences are typically deep-seated in their psyches and not always self-evident. However, these differences do result in certain behaviors that are typical of leaders and/or typical of managers. Table 3-1 is a side-by-side comparison of some of these typical differences.

Other researchers, such as Ronald Heifetz,[6] claim that managers and leaders are distinct in the processes they use to solve problems. For example, Heifetz claims that leaders typically use novel approaches to solve problems and handle conflict, and managers typically use existing precedent (or policy and procedure) to solve problems or handle conflict. It is clear that some of the earlier research on the differences between leadership and management is rooted in an indi-

TABLE 3-1	
COMPARISON OF COMMON LEADERSHIP AND MANAGEMENT BEHAVIORS	
TYPICAL LEADERSHIP BEHAVIORS	**TYPICAL MANAGEMENT BEHAVIORS**
Embraces conflict	Avoids conflict
Seeks to challenge process	Seeks a status quo
Seeks to understand chaos	Avoids chaos
Practices empathy	Practices sympathy
Uses interpersonal skills to solve problems	Uses policy and procedure to solve problems
Proactive	Reactive
Focus is on long-term goals	Focus is on short-term goals
Takes necessary risks	Seeks to avoid risks
Shares information freely	Treats information as "need to know"
Focuses on the opportunities	Focuses on the obstacles
Views problems as complex	Views problems as complicated
Emphasizes and rewards team performance	Emphasizes and rewards individual performance
Transformational behaviors	Transactional behaviors

vidual's philosophy of leadership, and perhaps even aspects of personality. However, it is necessary to understand that regardless of preference or personality, leadership and/or management can be learned. It has been argued that management is easier to learn than leadership because it is rooted in applying techniques. This may help to explain why there seems to be more managers in administrative roles.[6]

Understanding the Terms

When reading the literature relative to this question, it is important to recognize how the terms are generally understood. *Leadership* and *management* are references to behaviors and *leaders* and *managers* are references to people in specific positions or who hold a certain type of authority. Whereas leadership and management are a set of skills or techniques that anybody, regardless of their position or rank in an organization or society, can use given the proper motivation. That being the case, *leadership* constitutes a certain set of skills that anyone can acquire, develop, and utilize. Likewise, management can be described as different techniques anyone can utilize to increase efficiency. For example, leadership skills include empathy, initiative, contextual intelligence, interpersonal communication, future mindedness, strategic thinking, etc. Whereas management techniques includes budgeting, staffing, efficient use of technology, record-keeping, project management, etc. This is the basis for the commonly used axiom, *manage things, lead people.*

TABLE 3-2
MANAGEMENT AND LEADERSHIP VALUES

BENEFITS OF GOOD LEADERSHIP	BENEFITS OF GOOD MANAGEMENT
Fosters creative environment	Consistency and stability
Higher levels of mentorship	Clearly delineated boundaries
Flexible and resilient culture	Clearly understood expectations
Higher morale in the workplace	Delineated consequences for failure
Inspiring communication	Adequate checks and balances within the organizational structure
Greater sense of team and collaboration	Established interventions and assessments for commonly recurring problems
Freedom to learn from mistakes	Clear division of labor and responsibility

Basically, leadership consists of skills facilitating an individual's ability to influence and motivate people, teams, and groups to be better and accomplish more. Leadership behaviors are typically not constrained to specific methods. Management, on the other hand is when an individual engages in certain activities that increase the efficiency of people, teams, and groups. In contrast to leadership, management behaviors rely on consistent and repeatable methods. The irony here is that leadership behaviors seem to change from moment to moment, sometimes for no apparent reason despite effectiveness; whereas management behaviors rarely change despite ineffectiveness. Contemporary research on these 2 constructs is seeking to find ways to benefit from the strengths of both. It is also a commonly held belief that leadership is more desirable than management. This is not the case—both provide great value. Table 3-2 is a list of the values that management and leadership contribute.

The Difference According to Administrative Roles

Once we begin to talk about formal positions of authority like Chief Nursing Officer, Head Athletic Trainer, Director of Rehabilitation, Executive Director, Owner, Medical Director, etc—the lines begin to blur even further. The reason we lose some distinction is because good administrators practice both leadership and management. For example, it is not uncommon to refer to the Medical Director as a leader and a manager. However, this does not mean that the 2 constructs are synonymous. In fact, when we refer to them as a *leader*, we mean one thing—perhaps cutting-edge scholarship, selfless professional involvement, or inspiring behavior. When we refer to them as a *manager*, we tend to mean something else—perhaps reduction of medical errors or efficient processes. Something else that blurs the line between these 2 is that a majority of the nonclinical content spent in professional preparation involves learning management techniques (eg, budgeting, staffing, record-keeping) for "leadership" positions.

Discussion Questions

1. What are the major differences you have observed between someone you would consider a manager and someone you would consider a leader?
2. Do you believe that the primary differences between managers and leaders is a personality preference or something they have learned?
3. Which elements of your society or organization reward management behaviors over leadership?
4. Why do you think leadership is typically considered more desirable than management?
5. What management skills do you need to improve on?
6. What leadership skills do you need to improve on?

References

1. Algahtani A. Are leadership and management different? A review. *J Manage Policies and Practices.* 2014;2(3):71-82.
2. Shive M, Dorn B. Leadership versus management training in residency programs. *J Am Acad Dermatol.* 2012;67(4):789.
3. Day DV. Leadership development: a review in context. *Leadersh Q.* 2000;11(4):581-613.
4. Kotter JP. What leaders really do. *Harvard Bus Rev.* 2001;79:85-98.
5. Zaleznik A. Managers and leaders: are they different? *Clinical Leadership & Management Review.* 2003;18(3):171-177.
6. Heifetz RA. *Leadership Without Easy Answers.* Cambridge, MA: Harvard University Press; 1994.

QUESTION 4

So, I Want to Be a Better Leader— How Do I Develop a Philosophy of Leadership That Informs My Leadership Journey?

Eleanor Roosevelt said, "One's philosophy is not best expressed in words; it is expressed in the choices one makes."[1] That is so true, especially as it relates to leadership. For this question, I would like to take a decidedly less formal approach, but I want to start by asking a rhetorical question: *Do you need a philosophy of leadership?* It is rhetorical not because the answer is obvious, but because you already have one. That's right, everyone has a philosophy of leadership whether they are aware of it or not. It is as Mrs. Roosevelt implies, philosophies are seen in a person's actions and initially cannot always be articulated. However, we have a responsibility to articulate that philosophy once we are aware of it.

One of the most difficult aspects about leadership is being able to articulate a coherent and universal definition, but ironically, most people can accurately identify it when they see it. This is a very interesting paradox. While leadership is extremely difficult to define, it is relatively easy to spot. The reason for this, despite the nuances, is the underpinning philosophy of leadership that everybody has. At some level, that philosophy is similar enough between people that identifying leadership is fairly consistent. But, like anything in philosophy, articulating the reasons and rationality behind what we observe requires intentional effort.

In the previous questions we addressed what leadership is, why it is important, how it differs from management, and its outcomes. As you read those chapters and answered the discussion questions you likely found yourself agreeing or disagreeing with certain findings or commentary. The basis of those feelings about leadership are rooted in your philosophy of leadership. In fact, you have no real way of evaluating or critiquing what you hear or read about anything, let alone leadership, without first having a philosophy about it. You can think of your leadership philosophy as a filter you *always* use—sometimes intentionally and every other time unintentionally—to evaluate or critique leadership behavior of yourself or others.

If you consider yourself a lifelong learner, any reading, dialogue, or learning will inform your philosophy, which is always evolving. The best illustration of this is the old saying that a fish doesn't know it's in water until you take it out. The same is true with your philosophy of leadership—you don't know you have one until someone violates it. Therefore, we rarely pause to wonder or question what we think leadership is or why we think leadership is supposed to function a particular way. Ironically, the instant you realize that someone is not behaving like a leader, your philosophy of leadership is challenged, and only then is it brought to your awareness. Typically, instead of critically evaluating the rightness or wrongness of our philosophy of leadership, we deflect the uncomfortable possibility that our philosophy could be weak, and instead criticize the observed leadership behavior.

At this point we should ask what a philosophy is. A philosophy is a theory or belief held by a person that serves as a guiding principle for behavior and action. With this as our operating definition we can define a philosophy of leadership as the beliefs held by a person that inform his or her appreciation or criticism of leadership behaviors. Therefore, a philosophy of leadership is your understanding of the foundational nature of leadership. For example, it is common for people to assume that leadership is good, that leaders are valuable to society, and that people who demonstrate leadership get things done. These beliefs are rooted in a philosophy of leadership. The issue here is not you developing a philosophy of leadership—because whether you are aware of it or not you already have one—the issue is uncovering your philosophy and revealing the experiences that shaped it.

Ontology and Epistemology of Leadership

Being able to articulate a personal philosophy of leadership means that you can answer this question—what is it that I believe about leadership and does it stand up under scrutiny? A mature or developed philosophy of leadership must address the issues related to origin and essence (ontology) and development and demonstration (epistemology). *Ontology* is the study of being, or how something comes to exist. To have a mature philosophy of leadership, it is necessary to consider the origin of your personal leadership beliefs and experiences. You must ask yourself how did I come to understand leadership, and what experiences have I had that inform that belief. *Epistemology* is the study of knowledge, or how you come to know any particular thing. Related to a philosophy of leadership, epistemology addresses the issue of knowing what leadership is and how you recognize and identify it. Developing a philosophy of leadership requires asking ontological and epistemological questions that are summarized in Table 4-1.

A philosophy, which is not always consistent with someone else's philosophy, is alive, which means it changes; the ancient Greeks referred to this change as metamorphosis. As new information comes to light or new experiences are realized, the philosophy evolves. In this sense, a leadership philosophy is not static but dynamic. The difficulty with this or any philosophy is the personal nature of it. For example, what you consider to be horrible leadership, someone else may observe to be very good leadership. A philosophy of leadership is personal, in that it is always based on your own values, expectations, and experiences, but that does not mean your philosophy is mutually exclusive from others, or that it can ignore scrutiny or reject observed reality. Therefore, your philosophy of leadership must be attended to regularly. As we move through the rest of this book and embark on other questions related to leadership such as ethics, teamwork, organizational dynamics, and others—you will need to refer back to your philosophy of leadership and make adjustments.

Table 4-1	
Developing a Philosophy of Leadership	
ONTOLOGICAL QUESTIONS	**EPISTEMOLOGICAL QUESTIONS**
When did I first learn about leadership?	How do I know that someone is a leader?
What is the significance or purpose of leadership?	How do I know that leadership has just occurred?
Does leadership really matter to the big picture?	Is my understanding of leadership consistent with what others believe about leadership?
What early life experiences informed my understanding of leadership?	What are my assumptions about what leadership is?
What causes leadership to occur?	How do I know when there is an absence of leadership?
What behaviors do I attribute to leadership?	How do I distinguish leadership from similar constructs (eg, management, administration, supervision)?
At what point am I able to say confidently "I am a leader" irrespective of position or title?	What does one do to develop his or her leadership?

Discussion Questions

1. Do you believe leadership can be learned, or is it something an individual is just born with?
2. What is your earliest memory of seeing leadership in action firsthand?
3. What is your earliest memory of seeing firsthand a leadership failure?
4. What are 3 attributes that you always identify as absolute requirements for a good leader to demonstrate or possess?
5. At what point in your development, what has to have happened for you to introduce yourself to others as a leader?
6. Would your answer to question 5 change if you changed careers, lost your job, or lost your position?

Reference

1.   Eleanor Roosevelt Quotes. BrainyQuote.com, Xplore Inc, 2017, accessed October 26, 2017.

QUESTION 5

Do All Leaders Demonstrate Leadership Behaviors, and Is Everyone Who Demonstrates Leadership Behaviors a Leader?

As you might suspect, it is not quite that simple. Despite what many popular press books preach, not everyone can be a leader in a technical sense. The metaphor often used to support this is a "many-headed monster." For example, any single *thing* with more than one head is a monster. Obviously, companies and organizations cannot have more than one CEO, in fact, it is common practice for many organizations to have the CEO and president be the same person to avoid the "monster" scenario. Usually, what is meant when someone says everyone can be a leader is that anyone can practice or improve on specific leadership behaviors. In other words, not everyone can be a leader in the technical sense of organizational life, but everyone *can*—I would add they should practice leadership behaviors.

Delineating the Differences

In Question 3, we addressed differences between leadership and management. Most people would agree, especially in contemporary times, that the 2 are separate constructs. But it is more difficult to differentiate between a leader and leadership. In Question 4 we discussed having and developing a philosophy of leadership. Within that discussion we introduced ontology and episte- mology. These are 2 terms most often used and understood in the context of philosophy. Ontology is the nature and process of being. Epistemology is the science of knowing. To illustrate, asking, "Are you a leader," is an ontological question. The question, "How do you know you're a leader," is an epistemological question. For example, I can say, "I know I am a leader because in our organiza- tion I write the checks and make the difficult decisions," but that does not mean I am a leader in terms of intrinsic identity and value. It is entirely possible to not write checks and have no formal authority and still be the leader because of other factors.

The question that is before us now, *is there a difference between being a leader and practicing leadership*, is a philosophical extension related to ontology and epistemology. The idea being that one might practice leadership behaviors, but not yet be a leader. However, it is not possible to be a leader and not practice leadership behaviors.

Ontology is the issue when someone refers to himself, herself, or someone else as a leader regardless of position or rank. This is similar to the time when people begin to think of themselves as adults—that scary time when they think they might be, but aren't yet sure. This occurs at different times for different people based on their experiences, what they believe, and what they are told. Sometimes people refer to themselves as adults, and they technically might be, but deep down inside know that they are not, based on some conception, be it cultural, religious, or familial. Once this contradiction is resolved, sometimes taking years, they start becoming comfortable with their evolving identity. This doesn't mean there are never relapses—only that the behavior is generally consistent and reliable. Likewise, there comes a time for some people when they begin to think of themselves as a leader who is capable of leading beyond practicing leadership behaviors or role requirements. When a person genuinely begins to believe and realize they are a leader, they are becoming an "ontological leader."

The ontological perspective occurs when you begin to see yourself as a leader, which is confirmed epistemologically when others around you validate identity. Erhard et al[1] state that ontological leaders are people who do not think like leaders, but behave like leaders as a natural form of their self-expression. According to Erhard et al[1] the ontological leader doesn't turn on and off a leadership switch, but responds and acts spontaneously and intuitively as a leader to any situation that requires it.

Within the context of leadership development, there is a lot of debate and discussion over the issue of who can be a leader. It is a common understanding, at least in today's culture of leadership, that anybody can be a leader. In fact, it's difficult to find contemporary literature, empirical or theoretical, that states otherwise. I'm not here to contest that, but merely point out that those are 2 different things. Perhaps they are right in that anyone can be a leader, but that does not mean everyone is (even if they all wanted to be). As we have already established, there is only one CEO. It is one thing to say, "I am *the* leader," because I was duly elected to a formal position with a term limit or board oversight or because I make the schedule or set the agenda. It is another thing to say, "I am *the* leader " because I own or founded the company. And still, it is quite another thing to say, "I am *a* leader," because regardless of what is happing, my role, or the context, I can get us to where we need to be. The difference between the first example and the third is the difference between practicing leadership and being a leader. And, that distinction is a huge difference. The second example we need more information before we can determine what type of "leader-ness" is occurring. These 3 examples provide an explanation for why there is still so much to be learned about leadership, and why leadership research is so valuable to the constructs of culture and society.

The fact is, a leader who identifies as a leader and practices leadership behaviors as a reflex regardless of rank, title, position, or status is different from someone who demonstrates leadership behaviors because of role responsibilities. In reality, most people are "leaders" because of the latter. However, the path to *being* a leader, in the ontological sense, begins with or coincides with practicing leadership behaviors (Table 5-1).

TABLE 5-1

REASONS PEOPLE SAY THEY ARE A LEADER

THE "ONTOLOGICAL" LEADER	THE ROLE-BASED LEADER
I am a leader because I know I am. My leadership does not depend on rank, title, position, or status, but on my ability to solve problems and help people and organizations achieve their goals. Demonstrating leadership behaviors is a natural outcome that I expect of myself.	I am a leader because my role or job responsibilities require me to demonstrate certain leadership characteristics and behaviors. Demonstrating these leadership behaviors are contingent upon my job responsibilities and what other people expect of me.
I am a leader and want to contribute as a leader anywhere I can be effective or am needed, regardless if I have formal leadership responsibility are not.	I am only a leader in certain settings and am content to let other people lead when I have no formal responsibility.
Conviction-based, performs out of duty.	Competency based, performs out of obligation.

Note: Although the behaviors of these 2 types of leaders might be similar or even identical, that does not mean they are the same. The difference lies fundamentally in their perception of themselves, their place in society, and their philosophy related to leadership.

Ontology of Leadership in Health Care

The distinction between a role-based leader and an ontological leader has been introduced and studied empirically within health care. Kutz and Doherty-Restrepo[2] examined the frequency of leadership behaviors by athletic trainers within their athletic training roles and outside of their athletic training roles. They reported that athletic trainer's practice leadership significantly less when outside of their formal work responsibilities. Athletic trainers demonstrate leadership behaviors more frequently at work and significantly less outside of work. It is important to delineate that "outside of work" does not mean after hours in the pub or at home watching television, but in their other civic and social responsibilities outside of work. This finding lends strong support to the notion that athletic trainers, and perhaps other clinical professionals, are not ontological leaders, per se, and fall into the category of role-based leaders who think of leadership relative to rank, positions, title, and professional service. Kutz and Doherty-Restrepo[2] suggested that the absence of ontological leaders may be a limiting factor to professional growth and respect of athletic training. Within nursing, it has also been suggested that there is a need for more "ontological" leaders. Frilund[3] reported that nursing needs to develop an ontology of leadership so that future nurses can be prepared and know what processes are necessary for becoming nurse-leaders. Similar to athletic training, Frilund[3] recognizes that so much of the socialization of new nurses depends on learning and repeating role-based leadership behaviors, which are necessary at first, but seems to be lacking in the transference or integration of those behaviors into personal and professional identity.

Discussion Questions

1. At this stage in your career, how well do you believe you practice leadership behaviors?
2. Are you an "ontological" leader or a role-based leader? Why?
3. Personally speaking, what do you believe shows that someone is an "ontological" leader?
4. Do you believe you can be an "ontological" leader and not aspire to a formal rank or status within your organization or profession?
5. What leadership behaviors do you need to practice better to be considered a leader by others?

References

1. Erhard W, Jensen MC, Granger KL. Creating leaders: an ontological/phenomenological model. In: Snook S, Nohria N, Khurana R, eds. *The Handbook for Teaching Leadership.* Los Angeles, CA: Sage Publications; 2012:245-262.
2. Kutz MR, Doherty-Restrepo J. Frequency of Leadership Behaviors of Athletic Trainers in University Settings. *Athl Train Educ J.* In press.
3. Frilund M. Leadership ideas—a study with prospective nursing leaders. *Open J Nurs.* 2015;5(5):508.

SECTION II

QUESTIONS ABOUT LEADERSHIP DEVELOPMENT

QUESTION 6

Can Leadership Be Learned, and if so, How?

Learning Leadership?

Whether it's clinical skills, a foreign language, driving a car, riding a bike, or leadership, it is necessary to ask, how does learning occur? The learning process is not trivial and can get extremely complicated, especially with abstract and nuanced constructs like leadership. Contributing to the difficulty of learning leadership is how differently it is practiced and understood between people. There are so many diverse metrics and measurements of leadership, that deciding how to teach and assess it becomes very convoluted. Unfortunately, because of this difficulty, intentionally learning leadership is often neglected or relegated to chance.

Volumes have been written on learning theory, epistemology, and heuristics. Therefore, trying to answer this question obviously opens the Pandora's box of learning philosophy. Renowned learning theorists Kolb, Lewin, Piaget, Plato, Bloom, and Dewey among others, have contributed to this important issue. What they have provided to the scholarship of learning has helped advance modern education in many useful ways. Furthermore, convincing research on learning mindsets show, quite remarkably, that anyone can learn anything at any time, regardless of previous experience or belief about his or her aptitude.[1] With a robust history of learning theory and mindset research as a backdrop, the answer to *can* leadership be learned is absolutely yes! But, that is not our question. Our question is *how* is leadership learned? So, forgoing the scholarly framework of learning theory and carrying the assumption that leadership can be learned is how we will progress.

Lack of Leadership Education

Considering the outcomes of leadership (review Question 7) learning it can have a significant impact on an individual and an organization. As we've already established in previous chapters

Kutz MR. *Leadership Questions for Health Care Professionals: Applying Theories & Principles to Practice* (pp 21-36).
© 2018 SLACK Incorporated.

there is virtually no one, regardless of the field of inquiry, who is willing to say that leadership is not important. But ironically, research done in health care may indicate a disconnect. For example, Bellassai et al[2] reported 95% of physician assistant program directors believed that leadership is an important skill. However, only 45% of programs include leadership training as a part of their curriculum, and 67% of those include leadership training as a topic within another course. Only 11% offer leadership training as an independent course. Leadership development seems to be relegated or abdicated despite its importance. For example, Bellassai et al[2] reported most program directors stated that students are provided leadership opportunities through their clinical rotations, or through participating in extracurricular activities that promote leadership. Unfortunately, this is not unique to physician assistants. Indeed, this seems to be a trend with other health care professions as well. Nursing has reported the woeful lack of leadership development within their training[3]; medicine reports a need for leadership education in their curriculum[4]; and athletic training has also reported a similar need.[5] Within athletic training, the specific task of "manage[ing] human and fiscal resources by utilizing appropriate leadership" was reported to be the most difficult of all the tasks from all domains for which to write exam questions.[6] Therefore, despite being reported as extremely important and essential for success, leadership is the least evaluated in determining minimal competency.[6] In other health care disciplines, "nonclinical" roles of health care practitioners, including but not limited to leadership, are reported to be poorly addressed or to be less of a "concern" relative to clinical skill in health care education.[7,8,9] Obviously, there is a disconnect between the reported importance of leadership and its place in clinical and professional education.

Presumably any absence or deficiency of leadership education within health care appears to relate to the issue of *how* it can be learned. In fact, Cruz et al,[4] states that, despite the clear need for sound leadership, *how* to best train physician leaders is uncertain. In essence, leadership is believed to be important, but is not being taught adequately or at all because leadership competency and capability are difficult to measure accurately and reliably and takes more time to learn than clinical skills. Learning leadership appears to be relegated to on-the-job training, with the rather naïve assumption that the best leaders will rise to the top. Unfortunately, within organizations, it is not the cream that rises to the top, but the most ambitious. History is clear that the most ambitious are not always the most ethical or the most qualified to lead.

How Is Leadership Learned?

We have a paradox with on-the-job learning. Trial-and-error has been reported to be one of the best ways to learn anything, especially leadership.[10] However, that is based on the assumption the individual on-the-job is intending to learn to lead, which is an intentional process and not a passive one. Often times, the reality of on-the-job leadership development is the demand placed on those individuals in positions of authority that require a large amount of time and energy, and consequently, they end up foregoing the long and arduous task of formal leadership development. Therefore, the health care industry ends up having skilled clinicians in positions of authority who have little or no leadership ability or background. Consequently, the default, due to other demands, is to fall into a process of management that is primarily transactional. The research is clear that transactional leadership is least preferred and not as beneficial to morale and organizational culture as other styles of leadership (eg, transformational). Therefore, it is best to couple on-the-job leadership development with other more deliberate leadership development processes.

Kouzes and Posner[10] suggested that learning leadership occurs in 3 ways. The first, and some say the best way—but also the most difficult and sometimes most painful—is *trial-and-error*, which we already introduced. The second way to learn leadership is through *observation* of other leaders. This can be the observation of either successful leadership or failed leadership. It is sometimes said to be just as valuable to learn what not to do as it is to learn what to do. One common technique for this is through case study analysis. Another successful technique is direct observation of leadership in practice. The learner would observe and evaluate a leader in real time and describe, not only observed leadership behaviors, but also specific characteristics that they thought contributed to specific outcomes. Observation also includes how a leader's behaviors both influence and are influenced by follower's behaviors and contextual factors. The third way leadership can be learned is *formal education*. Formal education occurs through formal classroom work, readings, and the less formal, but often more intensive, leadership workshops or seminars. Often times, formal education is rich in theory and provides a foundational framework for values and beliefs, but often fails to provide a meaningful impartation unless coupled with observation and trial-and-error. To summarize, the best way to learn leadership is trial-and-error, but trial-and-error left to itself is too risky. Therefore, it is best to combine trial-and-error with one or both of the remaining methods, observation and formal education. This accelerates the leadership learning curve as well as protects the learner and the environment.

In addition to these 3 techniques, Mensch and Ennis[11] suggested 3 strategies for teaching that can be helpful in developing leadership programs:

1. **Use of scenarios and case studies.** This technique is of utmost importance and can help the learner use real-time scenarios and decision making to evaluate a variety of different leadership situations. The more you can make these cases and scenarios lifelike and pertinent to his or her actual job, the more likely leadership outcomes are realized.

2. **Authentic experiences.** This technique puts the learner in situations where the consequences are real but the potential damage is controlled. It is similar to trial-and-error, but more organized. These opportunities are created for the learner, but efforts have been taken to reduce—not eliminate—the uncertainty and volatility of most leadership situations. It is important that the learner feels some sense—although reduced—of consequence (negative and positive) for his or her actions when learning leadership.

3. **Positive educational environment.** Perhaps this goes without saying, but in an environment where leadership is being developed, it is important to provide feedback that is critical, positive, and goes beyond evaluating only demonstrated actions. The most valuable feedback will also explore a student's motives and attitudes relative to his or her leadership decisions. Feedback in the situation should come from both people in positions of authority, as well as the group or team to which the learner is responsible. Clear expectations should be established for success and failure.

Finally, Raelin[12] suggests that one of the biggest problems with contemporary leadership development is the association that leadership is learned by transferring instructions from experienced leaders, presumably those who know how to lead, to those who don't (eg, formal education). He suggests that this has been the operating model as far back as the 19th century, and that it simply has not worked—especially when used in isolation. Therefore, he makes the following recommendations for teaching leadership:

- Work-based developmental experiences: assign leadership responsibilities that have direct consequences and a relationship to the job(s) the learner is doing

- Peer mentoring: feedback should come from peers, as well as supervisors, and subordinates

- Leadership coaching: learner should be required to critically evaluate the intrinsic motivators of his or her leadership decisions and actions

- Apprenticeships: learner should practice leadership with experienced leaders

- Group process and reflection: leadership feedback should have group input

- Critical reflection of failure, dissonance, and crisis in the workplace: the best learning experiences are not always—in fact some believe rarely—from positive outcomes or feedback. Effectively learning leadership must include critical reflection of personal leadership failures.

- Action learning: participant stops and reflects on real time problems within his or her work environment

Discussion Questions

1. When is a time you remember learning a valuable leadership lesson? How has that lesson impacted your leadership?

2. Who is the best leader you have ever personally observed, and what made them the best? Is what made them the best reproducible in your own life?

3. Who is the best leader you have ever heard about or read about (fictional or real), and what made them the best? Is what made them the best reproducible in your own life?

4. What do you think you can do to be more intentional about learning leadership?

5. Why do you think leadership development is secondary in health care education?

6. Should leadership education be more prominent in entry-level health care education for every entry-level professional, or should it only be for more experienced clinicians who desire administrative or management roles within their organization or profession? Why or why not?

References

1. Dweck CS. *Mindset: The New Psychology of Success*. New York, NY: Ballantine Books; 2006.
2. Bellassai RJ, Glass CC, Halderson PE, Schoeberl JB. Leadership training in physician assistant programs: A survey of program directors. Paper presented at: 10th Annual Symposium on Graduate Research and Scholarly Projects; 2014; Wichita, KS.
3. Kelly LA, Wicker TL, Gerkin RD. The relationship of training and education to leadership practices in frontline nurse leaders. *J Nurs Adm*. 2014;44(3):158-163.
4. Cruz D, May Rose I, Hagiwara M, Canyon D. Systematic review of programs that enhance physician leadership. Paper presented at: Biomedical Sciences Symposium; April 2014; Honolulu, HI.
5. Kutz MR. A review and conceptual framework for integrating leadership into clinical practice. *Athl Train Educ J*. 2012;7(1):18-29.
6. Board of Certification, Inc. *Role delineation study and Practice Act*. Omaha, NE: Board of Certification, Inc; 2010.
7. Adamson BJ, Harris LM. Hunt AE. Health science graduates: preparation for the workplace. *J Allied Health*. 1997;26(4):187-199.
8. Cuppett M. Self-perceived continuing education needs of certified athletic trainers. *J Athl Train*. 2001;36(4):388-395.
9. Haverty C, Laham R. Empowering future athletic trainers: integrating evidence-based leadership into athletic training education programs. *Athl Train Educ J*. 2011;6(1):S8-S9.
10. Kouzes JM, Posner BZ. *The Leadership Challenge*. San Francisco, CA: Jossey-Bass Publishers; 1995.
11. Mensch JM, Ennis CD. Pedagogic strategies perceived to enhance student learning in athletic training education. *J Athl Train*. 2002;37(4 suppl):S199-S207.
12. Raelin JA. Rethinking Leadership. MIT Sloan Management Review Web site. 2015; 56(4);95-96. http://sloanreview.mit.edu/article/rethinking-leadership/. Published June 16, 2015. Accessed July 26, 2017.

QUESTION 7

So, What Happens When Someone Performs Leadership Behaviors Well?

Outcomes of Leadership

Our premise is that leadership is important and that it can be learned. Ultimately, the importance of leadership is based on valuable outcomes; without desirable outcomes it is difficult to say whether leadership has any importance beyond the esoteric. So, what are the benefits of leadership and why should you want to develop leadership skills? We will address these questions in 2 parts; the benefits of leadership to the larger community or organization; and then address how leadership impacts a profession and clinical practice by addressing how leadership positively influences patient outcomes.

Benefits of Leadership to Organizational Culture

Leadership is said to have positive and even profound benefits on the individual, the organization, and society.[1] This is generally well accepted, but it raises the question of what specific benefits? In a study of the US Army, Mumford et al[2] provides convincing evidence that people of different ages and from diverse backgrounds can learn to become better leaders. In this study, "better leader" was based on certain behaviors that were demonstrated more effectively after leadership education. Mumford et al[2] examined the leadership development of 1790 military officers from novice to expert and found that these 4 outcomes all significantly improved regardless of the level they previously demonstrated:

1. Leadership expertise (ie, knowledge of leadership)
2. Ability to solve complex problems
3. Creative thinking
4. Social judgment

While you would expect the first to be on the list, it is the other 3 that more directly address our question. This study supports the idea that leadership can be learned, but it also provides additional insight into how leadership can be measured. The measured outcomes contributes to being able to delineate beneficial outcomes of leadership. This does not mean that people without leadership cannot or do not demonstrate these outcomes, but it does suggest that when leadership is demonstrated, regardless of the role, position, age, or experience, these outcomes are seen more frequently. Therefore, leadership is said to contribute to being better able to solve complex problems, creatively generate new ideas, and engage in social judgment, which is the ability to evaluate an idea relative to current attitudes. Needless to say, these benefits can have a profound impact on organizational culture, individual performance, and even society.

One of the largest and most thorough systematic reviews of leadership consisted of 1161 empirical studies spanning 25 years. This study was conducted by Hiller et al[3] and they found that leadership has an important influence on 1) commitment and satisfaction, 2) perceptions, 3) motivation, 4) citizenship behaviors, and 5) behavioral processes. Again, these are large-scale constructs consisting of several sub-factors, but obviously represent a desirable impact on an individual, organization, and society. Their conclusion identified a significant benefit of leadership on organizational culture. For example, individuals who demonstrate leadership in organizations may be in a position to have a far greater impact within their community than compared to organizations with less of an emphasis on leadership. Individuals who demonstrate leadership behaviors are more likely to be engaged at work and contribute creative ideas. These 2 factors alone may have considerable return on investment for developing in practicing leadership. Hiller et al[3] identified specific criterion-based leadership outcomes based on their review (this is only a partial list):

- Increased effectiveness: this included sales growth, higher market valuations, increased revenue, better performance ratings, and increased creativity
- Better attitude: this included less cynicism, increased self-esteem, greater organizational commitment and satisfaction, higher trust, more motivation, and better emotional engagement
- Behavioral: this included more cooperation between coworkers, better communication, improved collaboration, and lower turnover
- Cognitive behaviors: increased perception of organizational support, better understanding of organizational structure, and improved workplace climate

In other words, when leadership is practiced 1) overall effectiveness is improved, 2) attitudes are markedly better, 3) colleagues behave better toward each other, and 4) there is an increased awareness and understanding of organizational goals. This does not mean that everyone who demonstrates leadership behaviors will have a positive impact on other individuals, their own performance, the organization, or their community; it only indicates that the probability is much higher. These were outcomes relative to leadership in general, but what about leadership behavior relative to health care?

Benefits of Leadership to Health Care and Patient Outcomes

Within health care, especially clinical practice, what are the benefits of leadership? First, let's address this question relative to professionalization and then address patient outcomes second. The National Research Council[4] defines professionalization as education that transforms a worker (or student) into a professional, and social processes by which an occupation becomes a profession. Leadership can both contribute toward the development of a student becoming a more respected professional as well as advance the reputation of a profession when professionals practice it. These can be pretty powerful outcomes, and are also worth the investment. An example of how that works is found in athletic training literature.

Kutz and Doherty-Restrepo[5] argue that one of the most compelling actions to promote professional recognition is leadership. Research on the frequency of leadership behaviors among athletic trainers indicates that athletic trainers do practice leadership-type behaviors within the context of their job, presumably because it is required at work, but sadly, they practice the same leadership behaviors significantly less when not at work. They argue that this is at least partly to blame for the relative unfamiliarity of athletic training as a health care profession.[5] The fact is, whether right or wrong, when leadership is practiced, observers perceive a greater sense of credibility and capability of the practitioner. Within health care, this can be highly advantageous, especially if you are trying to advance a profession. Within the context of student professionalization, research in nursing, medicine, and athletic training has demonstrated that students who develop leadership do better.

Nursing research[6] reports that nursing students who intentionally developed leadership behaviors acquired the following perceived beneficial outcomes:

- Better at prioritizing
- Enhancement of critical thinking skills
- Enhancement of technical skills (eg, clinical behaviors)
- Realization of peers as resources
- Development of management skills

Likewise, physician education and residency programs must be able to produce, not just outstanding clinicians, but outstanding clinician–leaders. Research within physician training has noted woeful inadequacies in how physicians are trained to practice nonclinical skills, which consists mostly of professional and leadership behaviors. Blumenthal et al,[7] suggest that residency training programs must teach nontraditional skills, such as how to engage in self-reflection, cultivate self-awareness, lead teams, practice "followership", lead change, negotiate, and develop and manage professional networks. Presumably, leadership training contributes towards these outcomes in medical students and residents. In fact, a low level of leadership adaptability was the primary contributing factor to lower exam scores of first-year medical students in a gross anatomy course.[8] Therefore, it is even possible that learning different leadership styles can improve class performance and ultimately grades. Finally, similar trends have been seen in athletic training education relative to student behaviors. Athletic training students who demonstrate leadership behaviors are more likely to be perceived as having better clinical skills.[9]

Pearson et al[10] conducted an extensive systematic review of nursing literature and reported a significant contribution of leadership behaviors toward a positive and healthy work environment. Nursing research has also shown a strong link between effective leadership styles and reduced staff burnout.[11] Shanafelt[12] found similar outcomes on the reduction of physician burnout associated with leadership behaviors of supervising physicians. With these findings it is relatively safe to conclude that one of the major contributors to reduced burnout among clinical health care professionals is effective leadership behaviors of both the supervisor and supervisee.

According to research in athletic training, nursing, and medicine, it is safe to draw the conclusion that leadership is in some way positively correlated to the perception of clinical competency and ultimately professional recognition. This is both exciting and dangerous. It is dangerous because leadership can be seen as a substitute for clinical skill, which it is not. I would never recommend forgoing mastery of clinical skills for the sake of leadership, in a misguided attempt to lead other people to believe you are better clinicians than you are. However, it is exciting because it implies that demonstrating leadership can be one way to meaningfully advance a profession. This is all good and well, but what about patient outcomes?

How does leadership impact patient outcomes? I have saved the best for last. Perhaps most exciting of all is that when leadership is practiced by clinicians, there seems to be compelling evidence that it contributes toward improved patient outcomes. The bulk of this work has been done in nursing. Nursing literature,[13] as well as medical literature, are clear that there are several positive outcomes associated with the practice of leadership. In a systematic review by Wong et al,[13] they reviewed 20 studies that showed a variety of positive relationships between different leadership behaviors and the following improved patient outcomes:

- Higher patient satisfaction
- Lower patient mortality
- Fewer medication errors
- Less restraint use
- Fewer hospital-acquired infections

Obviously, the key to realizing these kinds of outcomes is predicated on knowing which particular leadership behavior to use and when to use it. Therefore, leadership is not a panacea, but when used properly, and more importantly, when the practitioner develops a wide repertoire of leadership behaviors and styles, the likelihood of having a positive impact on patient outcomes is far more probable. Consequently, developing leadership awareness and skills can be a great way to improve personal satisfaction, organizational morale and performance, societal satisfaction, as well as advance and promote a profession and an individual within a profession, and perhaps most importantly, improve a variety of different patient outcomes. I know leadership sounds like a cure all, but it's not. However, leadership development is most definitely a worthwhile investment.

Discussion Questions

1. What benefits have you personally experienced as a result of practicing leadership-type behaviors?
2. How have you seen leadership behaviors be a benefit to teams or groups of which you have been a part?
3. How might practicing leadership better promote your profession in the local community?
4. Why do you think certain people practice leadership-type behaviors at work, but not outside of work?
5. If more health care professionals practiced leadership outside of work, do you think that might impact the perception of health care?
6. Have you seen or experienced leadership styles (good or bad) positively or negatively affect the work environment and staff burnout? How?

References

1. Black AM, Earnest GW. Measuring the outcomes of leadership development programs. *Journal of Leadership & Organizational Studies.* 2009;16(2):184-196.
2. Mumford MD, Marks MA, Connelly MS, Zaccaro SJ, Reiter-Palmon R. Development of leadership skills: experience and timing. *Leadersh Q.* 2000;11:87–114.
3. Hiller NJ, DeChurch LA, Murase T, Doty D. Searching for outcomes of leadership: a 25-year review. *Journal of Management.* 2011;37(4):1137-1177.
4. National Research Council. *Professionalizing the Nation's Cybersecurity Workforce? Criteria for Decision-Making.* Washington, DC: The National Academies Press; 2013.
5. Kutz MR, Doherty-Restrepo J. Frequency of Leadership Behaviors of Athletic Trainers in University Settings. *Athl Train Educ J.* In press.

6.   Bos S. Perceived benefits of peer leadership as described by junior baccalaureate nursing students. *J Nurs Educ.* 1998;37(4):189-191.

7.   Blumenthal DM, Bernard K, Bohnen J, Bohmer R. Addressing the leadership gap in medicine: residents' need for systematic leadership development training. *Acad Med.* 2012;87(4):513-522.

8.   Pawlina W, Hromanik MJ, Milanese TR, Dierkhising R, Viggiano TR, Carmichael SW. Leadership and professionalism curriculum in the gross anatomy course. *Anals-Academy of Medicine Singapore.* 2006;35(9):609.

9.   Kutz MR. Leadership is positively related to athletic training students' clinical behaviors. *Athl Train Educ J.* 2012;7(3):95-102.

10. Pearson A, Laschinger H, Porritt K, Jordan Z, Tucker D, Long L. Comprehensive review of evidence on developing and sustaining nursing leadership that fosters a healthy work environment in health nursing care. *Int J Evid Based Healthc.* 2007;5(2):208-253.

11. Wong CA, Cummings GG. The influence of authentic leadership behaviors on trust and work outcomes of health care staff. *Journal of Leadership Studies.* 2009;3(2):6-23.

12. Shanafelt TD, Gorringe G, Menaker R, et al. Impact of organizational leadership on physician burnout and satisfaction. *Mayo Clin Proc.* 2015;90(4):432-440.

13. Wong CA, Cummings GG, Ducharme L. The relationship between nursing leadership and patient outcomes: a systematic review update. *J Nurs Manag.* 2013;21(5):709-724.

Question 8

I Heard Leading Is Difficult—Does Practicing Leadership Generate, or Reduce, Stress?

Outcomes of Leadership

It is a common assumption and generally understood that being a leader can be extremely stressful. In fact, it is not uncommon for people to turn down or avoid leadership positions because of the presumed stress it may cause. In this response, I want to use existing evidence to challenge that assumption. To really get at the root of this we need to understand if leadership is more stressful than an alternate position. If we use the patient/problem, intervention, comparison, outcome (PICO) model for framing a clinically-relevant question for this assumption, it might read as follows (here are a few examples):

- In people who hold stable leadership positions, is there a higher level of stress compared to people who do not hold leadership positions?
- Does having a stable leadership position create more stress, as measured physiologically by increased cortisol levels and psychologically by higher anxiety, when compared to people in the same organization without a leadership position?
- Do leaders experience higher levels of negative stress than nonleaders?

When we frame the question using the PICO model, it forces us to examine our presumption that leadership is *more* stressful than something else. Notice, by using a clinically-relevant question, we have taken the question out of the general, *is leadership stressful*, to which there is no context and therefore cannot be accurately answered, to a more appropriate context-based approach, which asks if it is more stressful than some comparator under certain conditions? With this new frame of reference we can now begin to explore what the relevant empirical research reports on the question.

Believe it or not, there is significant empirical evidence that addresses this issue. To begin, research on nonhuman primates suggests that cortisol levels in dominant apes were significantly less than nondominant apes.[1,2,3] While these studies do not address our question specifically (eg, humans) the observation led an elite research team from Harvard (Cambridge, Massachusetts), University of California (Berkeley, California), and Stanford University (Stanford, California) to explore if this was also seen in humans.[4] This does address our question specifically. As it turns out after a rigorous experimental design (I would encourage you to look up the referenced article and read it) organizational leaders have significantly less salivary cortisol (physiological indicator of stress), and less reported anxiety compared to nonleaders. The finding indicates both a physiological and psychological advantage to leadership relative to reduced levels of stress. Sherman et al[4] extended their initial findings by exploring if leadership-stress relationship is affected by the leader's sense of control. To do that, they looked to see if there was a difference in the level of stress between leaders with 1) a high number of subordinates, 2) leaders with a high number of direct reports, and 3) leaders with a high level of authority.

Two of the groups, leaders with a high level of subordinates and those with a high degree of authority was predictive of less stress. However, leaders with a high number of direct reports was not predictive and nonsignificant. In other words, leaders with a high number of subordinates and or a high degree of authority have less stress. Leaders with a high number of direct reports did not—they experienced higher (or normal) amounts of stress, both psychologically and physiologically. They attributed this to the fact that having a high number of direct reports does not contribute to a sense of control over the environment.

The difference between subordinates and direct reports is important. Subordinates are employees who must follow instructions and fall at a lower rank on the organizational chart (in other words are not a threat to you), rarely give feedback, and are rarely considered peers, per se; whereas direct reports may be peers (or staff) who are directly accountable to you but can challenge or disagree and can be seen as a threat to your position. Stated another way, more colloquially, subordinates rarely look for organizational loop holes or try and "go over your head" when a decision does not fall in their favor; however, direct reports are perceived to "go over your head" or find loop holes around your authority.

These findings have at least 2 meaningful implications. First, it provides additional evidence relative to any difference between management and leadership. As having direct reports tends to be more indicative of management-type positions and skills (ie, organizing and controlling the actions and outcomes of a diverse group of people). Secondly, it shows how context and the nature of the relationships you have with your coworkers has a dramatic effect on leadership and stress. One particular point of interest is that this particular research is less about a leader's rank (or position) and more about a leaders sense of control over his or her environment.

The implication is that those leaders who have a high degree of control over their environments have both physiological and psychological benefits in lower levels of stress. Relative to this research, we could assume that individuals with a certain amount of control, whether they are formal leaders or not, may also benefit from lower levels of stress. Managers, however, who interact in an environment with peers and direct reports, who are not necessarily their subordinates, and therefore have less control over their environment, are likely to experience higher levels of stress compared to leaders with a higher sense of control.

It is plausible that holding a leadership position of any kind may increase the sense of control, which is a stress buffering response and alters physiological and psychological consequences resulting in lower cortisol levels and anxiety. This means that the adverse effects on health that comes from job strain and uncertainty can be managed effectively by demonstrating leadership, which contributes to a greater sense of control over your job and career. However, these findings are predicated on the stability of the position. For example, if leadership is in an organization or industry that is highly volatile and unstable, the stress mitigating consequence of leadership may not be as apparent or even absent. Research still needs to be done that examines stress response and leadership in industries where there is less control and higher volatility, such as health care.

Regardless, leadership is a significant predictor of both cortisol and anxiety when you control for sex, age, education, income, and mood.[4] It is also important to note that the greater level of authority an individual had over subordinates predicted a greater sense of control which in turn resulted in even less stress. This indicates that the higher one ascends within an organization, in terms of organizational hierarchy in authority, stress becomes less and not greater. This may be counterintuitive to many of us, but when considered relative to control makes sense.

Leadership Control in Health Care

It is well accepted that the health care industry is one of the most complex and unstable environments around the world. Whether it's in the United States or other countries with socialized or public medicine, that does not change. Health care is an extremely complex environment. Consequently, it is worth asking if the same stress mitigating effects of leadership will carry over into environments such as health care. It is interesting to note that managing a large number of people is not associated with control or less stress. What is interesting about this is that there seems to be no correlation to management positions or management-type behaviors with decreased stress, but in fact, the difference between levels of stress may be dependent upon differentiating between management and true leadership.

Implications for Health Care

As we have mentioned, the jury is out concerning the leadership-stress relationship within the context of health care. Two unique things distinguish the Sherman and colleagues[4] study to the context of health care. First, given the uncontested understanding that health care is one of the most complex, volatile, and uncertain organizational environments, it is not an exaggeration to assume a sense of control is a luxury. It is certainly not impossible, but definitely a rarity. Secondly, most health care workers, especially clinicians, work with direct reports, instead of subordinates. For example, athletic trainers, nurses, physical therapists, physicians, exercise physiologists, and physician assistants may report to each other, but do not serve as anyone's direct supervisor. These 2 factors warrant considerable caution when interpreting these results to health care leaders. However, based on the best available evidence, it can be said with a degree of certainty that leaders in general, and more specifically people with a sense of control over their environment, experience significantly less stress comparatively.

Discussion Questions

1. Have you ever thought to yourself that leaders have more or less stress?
2. What assumptions contributed to your answer to the previous question?
3. Have you ever considered that your sense of control correlates to the amount of stress you experience?
4. What do you think about the notion that essentially more responsibility equates to less stress? (Remember, this is not someone's theoretical idea, but a statement based on the best available evidence.) How might you justify this to your observed experience?

5. What are some things you can do immediately to begin to experience greater control over your environment?
6. Do you think that the finding by Sherman and colleagues[4] is generalizable to health care?

References

1. Sapolsky RM. Hypercortisolism among socially subordinate wild baboons originates at the CNS level. *Arch Gen Psychiatry*. 1989;46:1047-1051.
2. Sapolsky RM. Social subordinance as a marker of hypercortisolism. Some unexpected subtleties. *Ann N Y Acad Sci.* 1995;771:626-639.
3. Sapolsky RM. The influence of social hierarchy on primate health. *Science.* 2005;308:648-652
4. Sherman GD, Lee JJ, Cuddy AJ, et al. Leadership is associated with lower levels of stress. *Proceedings of the National Academy of Sciences of the United States of America.* 2012;109(44):17903-17907.

QUESTION 9

Leadership Is an Old Construct, With Many Different Ideas Attached to It— How Has Leadership Evolved Over Time?

Another distinction between management and leadership is their ages. It is generally understood that management is a concept invented around the Industrial Revolution, and became a focus of research in the 1800s. However, leadership has been a topic of fascination from antiquity. In fact, several attempts to date when it first appeared in ancient writings have failed, suffice to say, it dates back several thousand years BC.

Just like anything else that evolves over time, leadership has changed dramatically over the centuries. In fact, when examining ancient writings about leadership, it is difficult to reconcile how we understand it today. Obviously, there is (and always will be) a universal or even innate understanding of what leadership is. As we discussed in earlier chapters, identifying when people are demonstrating leadership behaviors is relatively easy, but defining it succinctly has proven to be difficult. Part of that difficulty is due to the fact that leadership changes as cultures and societies change. "Different generations have different expectations of leadership and how a good leader has to be."[1] Given these differences, and the gradual change, it is important to understanding how leadership has evolved so that we can attempt to predict what it might look like in the future. This will have a profound impact on leadership development, as well as professional socialization, and even formal education programs.

Generally speaking, there have been 4 major paradigms relative to how leadership has been understood throughout history (Figure 9-1). Those are classical models, transactional models, visionary models, and organic models.[2] These 4 models are typically used by organizations and individuals as a lens through which to evaluate leadership effectiveness. Therefore, it is critical that we understand each lens. Ironically, different individuals still default to certain lenses based on their personality, experiences, and training. This means that in any one context, different people are using different lenses. Therefore, for the health care professional to be effective, he or she needs to understand that at any given time he or she is being evaluated based on criteria from any one of these or any combination of these 4 models. This adds an incredible amount of complexity to demonstrating leadership efficiently.

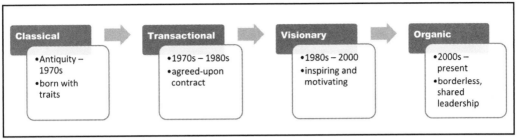

Figure 9-1. Evolution of leadership thinking.

Evolution of Leadership Models

The first paradigm is the *classical model* and is by far the longest standing ideology. The classical model dates from antiquity up until the 1970s.[2] As such, this model is deeply rooted in the psyche of many leaders and deeply intertwined within organizational and civic cultures. The classic leadership model (also referred to as trait theory) is the idea that great leaders are usually men or women who were part of a special group or class of people deserving or destined to lead. It is the classical model that is responsible for the common belief that leaders are born, not made. In the early 1900s a major focus of research was devoted to uncovering what these traits were.

The second model is referred to as *transactional leadership*. Transactional leadership was prominent from the 1970s to the 1980s, nearly 2 decades. It became popular with the advent of a relatively new concept called management. The transactional model is based on a formal transaction between a subordinate and supervisor, generally called a *contract*. The transactional model was implemented to create a predictable and patterned environment, and required the leader to be an expert technician who supervised nonexpert technicians. It is this model that is responsible for the assumption that leaders know more, and are, consequently, more qualified than the general public.

The third model is called *visionary leadership*. This model grew in popularity from the mid-1980s up until around the early 2000s. Visionary leadership (also referred to as *transformational*) is particularly useful in turbulent times, and it was developed to create consensus and momentum among the workforce. This was a significant change from transactional thinking, where leaders changed from forcing or manipulating followers to complying for the good of the company to inspiring and motivating followers. The major emphasis in the visionary model was on the leader's ability to inspire people to better perform, where "better" was mutually agreed-upon by the leader and follower. It was in the visionary model that referring to workers as "subordinates" became unpopular, and was replaced with the more benign term "follower."

The fourth model is the *organic model*. This model dates from early 2000's to the present. Organic leadership understands that the organization is alive, it is a living entity capable of growing, and self-organizing. Within the organic model, leaders typically prefer the term facilitator, and organizational leadership is developed from within the organization, or at a grassroots level. Another very interesting aspect of the organic model is that leadership is generally shared and traditional hierarchical structures are avoided. This model was popularized with the advent of knowledge workers. Today's workforce is highly specialized and highly educated requiring a different styles of leadership.

Discussion Questions

1. Of the 4 evolutionary leadership models, which do you find yourself most attracted to, and why?

2. How would you handle a supervisor who believes strongly in one model, peers who believe in a second model, and yourself who functions out of a third model?

    a. Note, this is not uncommon. Several organizations have owners and supervisors who operate out of the classical model, mid-level managers who are transactional or visionary, and new or young professionals who are organic.

3. How does the mixture of these 4 models influence the efficiency and growth of your work environment?

References

1. Frilund M. Leadership ideas—a study with prospective nursing leaders. *Open J Nurs.* 2015;5(5):508.
2. Avery G. *Understanding Leadership.* London, United Kingdom: Sage Publications; 2005.

SECTION III

QUESTIONS ABOUT TEAMWORK AND COMMUNICATION

QUESTION 10

Teamwork Is Important—So, What Do I Need to Do to Be a Valuable Contributor to My Team?

There is very little debate about the necessity of teamwork within health care. In fact, the Institute of Medicine[1] says that working on interdisciplinary teams is a fundamental competency for health care professionals. And, I dare say that almost every individual discipline within health care states explicitly, or at least has an implicit expectation, that teamwork is a fundamental competency for its members. In fact, interdisciplinary health care teams engaged in direct patient care have been shown to have dramatic impact on improving clinical outcomes for patients.[2] Therefore, it is imperative that clinical professionals, regardless of discipline, learn how to contribute to and be a valuable member of a team.

The Most Important Teamwork Behavior

A quick Google search on behaviors of an effective team member yields over 22 million hits. Therefore, it is safe to assume there is no shortage of opinion concerning what it takes to be a valuable contributor to a team. Each list undoubtedly ranks the importance of team member behaviors, and when there are many lists, there are bound to be contradictions. In other words, there are probably several different "most important" team member behaviors. However, I would like to remind you that you do not have an inalienable right to be on a team simply because you are part of a workgroup. Being a member of a professional organization, earning a degree, or being hired to do a job does not give you the right to be on a team. You may be given the benefit of the doubt at the beginning, but you must earn your right to stay a contributing member. You earn your right to be on the team for no other reason than exceptional clinical practice. If you do not perform your job well and competently, do not expect to be considered a valuable member of any team. Doing your job consistently well is the most important behavior of a valuable team member. Once you have demonstrated that you can do your job well, there are other behaviors that are necessary in order to add value to your team.

Kutz MR. *Leadership Questions for Health Care Professionals: Applying Theories & Principles to Practice* (pp 39-62).
© 2018 SLACK Incorporated.

Why Contribute to a Team?

There are many lists that delineate what members of teams ought to do in order to contribute, but first, we must address why contributing to a team is important. Contributing to a team not only improves team morale; it can help improve patient outcomes and add a significant amount of personal satisfaction to your work. The things that you can do to successfully contribute to a team are not personality dependent, anybody with any personality can contribute to a team. From an employer's standpoint, having a cohesive team increases retention, encourages innovation, and reduces job dissatisfaction, which has a significant impact on revenue and time lost. Effectively contributing to a team has a significant impact on the bottom line and job satisfaction.

Valuable Team Members' Behaviors

Obviously, there are many dynamics that contribute to the success of a team. However, there are specific individual contributions that must be made by each team member. Michan and Rodger[3] reviewed the literature and identified 4 key contributions individuals must make on teams. Those contributions are 1) self-knowledge, 2) trust, 3) commitment, and 4) flexibility.

Each team member must possess self-knowledge. Team members that do not possess self-knowledge will seriously hinder team success. Self-knowledge includes an accurate awareness of your own skills and responsibilities in relation to others on the team. Self-knowledge requires rejecting the temptation to be envious of another team member's roll, skills, or capacity. Self-knowledge includes understanding what skills you have and how those skills fit relative to every other team member's contributions. An important aspect of self-knowledge is honesty about any limitations in your skills. It is not necessarily damaging to have weaknesses in your skills, it only becomes so when you fail to recognize or acknowledge them. Self-knowledge also includes being able to clearly articulate expectations, specifically, expectations you have of yourself relative to the team. In other words, valuable team members articulate how their skills add value—this includes having a positive self-image, which was seen to be a significant contribution by other team members.

Trust is also an important aspect of contributing to a team. According to Michan and Rodger,[3] trust originates from self-knowledge and competence. You can only give trust when you yourself are competent and are acutely aware of your own ability and limitations. Trust is a consequence of reliability. When you show yourself reliable—consistently repeating the same behaviors over and over—trust is a natural outcome. Trust, as described by Michan and Rodger,[3] does not only mean that you must be trustworthy—that is implied—but, to be a valuable member of the team you must be willing to trust others. Commitment is another behavior that valuable team members demonstrate. Michan and Rodger[3] state that the building blocks for commitment are the ability to trust others and accurate self-knowledge. The best way to demonstrate commitment is to make short-term personal sacrifices. Without commitment, team members will not make sacrifices. Without this level of commitment it is virtually impossible to achieve any sort of motivation or direction. In other words, to be a valuable team member you must be willing to show your commitment to the team by being willing to make personal sacrifices for the sake of the team's goals.

Finally, team members must be flexible. Flexibility is the ability to maintain an open attitude, accommodate different personal values, and be receptive to the ideas of others.[3] Without flexibility, team members will make inappropriate and often inaccurate assumptions about their colleagues. Flexibility in this case is not about resilience or adaptability, per se, but about being open-minded to diverse experiences and ideas. This kind of flexibility allows for innovation and creativity, which is a hallmark of successful teams. Without flexibility, team members cannot be valuable contributors because they will most likely hinder progress by requiring the team to function only in ways in which they are familiar or comfortable.

Contributing During Conflict

There is absolutely no question that conflicts will happen. No team is immune to conflict. Regardless of how high the morale, or selfless the behavior, conflict is inevitable. One of the most important things you can do to be a valuable team member is to not hold conflict against other members of your team. Accept conflict as part of the process and always be willing to give the benefit of the doubt. If you truly embrace the behaviors of a good teammate—self-knowledge, trust, commitment, and flexibility —any conflict can be overcome.

Discussion Questions

1. What characteristics would you say make for successful team members?
2. What skills do you have that add the most value to the teams you are on?
3. Think of a team that you belong to. Was there ever a time when your lack of flexibility (open-mindedness) hindered the team's goal? What was it? What would you do differently today?
4. What short-term personal sacrifices have others around you made for the sake of the team that caused you to admire them? Why do you think they made that sacrifice for the team?
5. How willing are you to give trust to someone new?
6. It takes time to develop a cohesive team, and trust is a critical part of that, but most of the time trust must be given before it is earned. Do you agree with that statement, and how easily do you trust other members of your team?

References

1. Institute of Medicine Committee on the Health Professions Education Summit. *Health Professions Education: A Bridge to Quality.* Washington, DC: National Academies Press; 2003.
2. Chisholm-Burns MA, Lee JK, Spivey CA, et al. US pharmacists' effect as team members on patient care: systematic review and meta-analyses. *Med Care.* 2010;48(10):923-933.
3. Michan S, Rodger S. Characteristics of effective teams: a literature review. *Aust Health Rev.* 2000;23(3):201-208.

I Get Along Great With Most of My Colleagues, but How Do I Navigate Difficult Coworker Relationships?

Navigating difficult and hostile coworkers can be extremely stressful. Many studies have documented the increasing prevalence of incivility in the workplace.[1] This increase in workplace incivility has been attributed to multiple issues such as re-engineering, downsizing, budget cuts, productivity, and cycle-time improvement. Adding to those stresses, the workforce has become significantly more diverse with greater cultural and language differences, different work styles inherent among various generations and nationalities, and with increasing use of a temporary workforce.[1] These complex variables come together to create workplace dynamics where getting along is not always possible and misunderstandings are more probable.

Despite its ease, ignoring difficult coworkers is not effective. In this chapter, we will explore useful ways to handle coworkers who, despite our best efforts, refuse to be reasonable. Before listing any solutions, we must first explore 2 basic rules of thumb (also known as heuristics) relative to working with difficult people.

We all know that working with difficult people cannot be avoided. Unfortunately, within health care, this risk seems to be higher than normal. Sofield and Salmond[2] reported that 91% of orthopedic nurses in their sample had experienced verbal abuse within the last month, and physicians were the most frequent abusers. Given the unique power distances between various health care professionals and the high level of cultural diversity within the health care industry, the increased risk should not be surprising. However, health care professionals must still use the rules of thumb in dealing with challenging coworkers.

The first rule of thumb is to know your role in the problem. When it comes to unreasonable coworkers, consider how you may have contributed. Do not rule out the possibility that you are a contributor to the difficulty. It is wise to reflect on your own behavior before you conclude that it is entirely the other party who is being unreasonable. Ask yourself if you have done or said anything that could possibly have been misunderstood. The second rule of thumb is to remember what most of us learned as a child about "being nice." Or, stated another way, practice the "golden rule." When dealing with difficult people always remember to treat others the way you would like to be treated. These 2 approaches often significantly help reduce the kind of stress and tension associated with working with difficult colleagues. However, these 2 behaviors do not always work. When they do not, the literature has provided some best practices to employ.

Literature Best Practices for Working With Difficult People

Solomon[3] identifies 5 types of difficult colleagues, raging bulls, tacklers, enviers, squelchers, and intimidators. Raging bulls erupt unexpectedly in a fit of rage. The best way to handle raging bulls is to leave immediately and re-engage only after they have calmed down or have had a chance to vent. It is important to know when dealing with raging bulls that you should not try to analyze their behavior or take it personally. If you know someone is prone to erupt, it is always advantageous to have solutions at the ready when delivering potentially difficult information.

Tacklers are colleagues who are prone to personally attack you when they feel threatened or surprised. The best way to handle tacklers is avoid immediately taking offense, realize their frustration is based on being surprised, and is not necessarily directed at you, then calmly inform them that they do not need to get personal. Ask them to offer any suggestions they might have to resolve any personal conflicts. It is also important to continue with your game plan. Do not let tacklers lure you into groveling and apologizing for what they accused you of (unless of course you did antagonize them). Try and steer the conversation away from personal issues back toward the task at hand.

Enviers are colleagues who begrudge or resent you because of the praise and accolades you receive. When dealing with colleagues who may be envious, it is important that you let your work speak for itself and never fall to the temptation to justify why you deserved recognition. Never belittle or condescend. Enviers need to be encouraged, not flattered, and you should always convey that the process is fair and each person's work is judged on its own merit. The proverbial wisdom with these types of colleagues is to "take the high road."

Squelchers consist of colleagues who dismiss or crush any opinion that is not theirs. They are particularly hostile toward novel ideas that they did not come up with. When dealing with squelchers it might be necessary to find support from other victims. You should never find allies in an attempt to gang up on another coworker, but you can find allies for solace. Stand your ground and reiterate that ideas are evaluated on their merit—not their owner. Regardless of the owner, it is important to encourage a responsible critique of ideas that must be accompanied by validated evidence. Give squelchers the benefit of the doubt. Doing that will help you better prepare and critique your own ideas. It is also important to note that squelchers often times presume that new ideas haven't been vetted properly. This belief, true or not, contributes to their hyper criticism. So, it is fair to consider that any opposition may not be personal, per se, only that they believe they see what you don't. Therefore, squelchers can be silenced best when you are prepared with a list of merits and flaws for a new idea. This will help calm their unease and convey the idea (and confidence) that you also have a broad vantage point.

Lastly, some employees are intimidators. Intimidators try to gain support by implying (rarely are they explicit) that they can harm or embarrass you in some way. They typically don't go so far as explicit blackmail, but they may hold certain information as a way to manipulate. Despite their attempts to make you feel inferior, it is important that you understand your role and contribution to the workplace. One of the most effective things you can do is refuse to let them frazzle you. You can do this by rehearsing rebuttals at home (role-play your retorts with a trusted friend). Consistently present yourself as poised, calm, and confident. Proverbial wisdom that applies here would include the old axiom, never let them see you sweat. Also, be sure you know when to laugh it off. Sometimes intimidating behavior is not meant to be intimidating, but is only an informal hazing, which once understood correctly is actually a form of acceptance (that doesn't make it right, but it does reduce the tension). Finally, as a summary—never retaliate. Despite the temptation, despite what they earn or deserve, do not retaliate, and let your attitude and quality speak for itself.

In addition to the above recommendations, Whitaker[4] cites the following recommendations for dealing with passive-aggressive coworkers. I would offer this as a sixth type. Passive-aggressive coworkers are nonresponsive and avoid confrontation. Their fault is indirect resistance to the demands of others, and takes the form of procrastinating, pouting, or "losing" important materials. Ways you can deal with passive-aggressive coworkers include:

- Clarify expectations: be sure as many nuances as possible are explicitly stated and agreed-upon before a project begins.
- Measure results: once expectations are stated, expect results. If a mistake is made, expect more than an apology, expect the next project to be done at or above standards.
- Acknowledge the merits of a complaint: if issues are raised, be sure to evaluate fairly.
- Avoid defensiveness: do not automatically dismiss claims that you believe are unfounded.
- Challenge distortions or half-truths: when a claim is found to be distorted or unreliable, you must confront and correct the distortion, not the individual's behavior.

In short, never allow passive-aggressive behavior to be tolerated. Mistakes happen and certain personalities are less confrontational than others. However, if someone is intentionally sabotaging progress, that must be addressed by the team.

As an aside, it is important to note that my advice, or the literature that I have summarized previously from Solomon[3] and Whitaker,[4] is not legal advice. And for sure, harassment of any kind or workplace bullying should be taken seriously, and if deemed a threat, should be taken to human resources for a full investigation. However, the intent of handling difficult colleagues is to first show yourself as a good colleague and give the benefit of the doubt. However, if you have tried to give the benefit of the doubt, and turned the other cheek, so to speak, and difficult behavior persists, get a second opinion from human resource personnel.

Discussion Questions

1. Without naming names, what was the most difficult coworker behavior you have ever had to deal with?
2. Taking into consideration your own personality, what are a few ways that you believe you could best handle different types of difficult coworkers identified in this chapter?
3. What are some other ways not listed here that you feel would be beneficial in dealing with difficult coworkers?
4. Discuss how being the best at what you do and consistently improving your skills mitigate some of the challenges that difficult coworkers bring.

References

1. Yeung A, Griffin B. Workplace incivility: does matter in Asia? *People & Strategy.* 2008;31(3):14-20.
2. Sofield L, Salmond SW. Workplace violence: a focus on verbal abuse and intent to leave the organization. *Orthop Nurs.* 2003;22(4):274-283.
3. Solomon M. *Working With Difficult People: Revised and Expanded.* New York, NY: Prentice Hall; 2002.
4. Whitaker C. Career path. Passive-aggressive colleagues: dealing with difficult behavior. *Nursing.* 2000;30(6):82-83.

QUESTION 12

I Know Change Starts With Me— How Do I Begin to Develop Good Relationships With Coworkers?

Workplace relationships are important, and most people understand that in order to be a contributing member of a team they must work at it. This is especially true in health care where teams can be extremely diverse. It is not uncommon for one work team to consist of physicians, nurses, athletic trainers, physical therapists, occupational therapists, and a multitude of medical technicians (eg, x-ray techs, phlebotomists, medical assistants). In this chapter, we will briefly introduce a few behaviors that can go a long way in developing positive workplace relationships, regardless of the multiplicity of team member's experience, background, and education.

Humans are naturally social creatures. Considering the amount of time most people spend at work, it is not uncommon to want to feel a sense of community and connection with colleagues. Many employers look to create this dynamic by creating a common vision and purpose. While this is important, it is not necessarily what motivates individual employees. Research reveals a sharp contrast between job satisfaction and organizational commitment.[1] Ignoring this difference is huge and sometimes leads to well-intentioned, but misguided "team development" activities. For example, most organizations are interested in organizational commitment and consequently develop programs and policies accordingly. In contrast, most employees are interested in job satisfaction, which often is haphazardly grouped in with organizational commitment. This tension between organizational commitment and personal job satisfaction can generate stress. While many managers place organizational commitment first, it is likely that job satisfaction is an antecedent to organizational commitment (not vice versa). Job satisfaction can be greatly enhanced by having a good working relationship with colleagues.

Good Workplace Relationships

There are several benefits to having good working relationships; not the least of which is higher morale, innovation, greater energy, and emotional engagement. In fact, support from colleagues is one of the number one predictors of workplace performance and employee engagement.[2]

In other words, when colleagues feel connected and supported by the people they work with, not just their supervisors, they are more likely to engage in their workplace and their work-related outcomes improve.

Good workplace relationships are generally contingent on the following characteristics[3]:

- Trust
- Respect
- Open-mindedness
- Clear communication

Trust is the foundation of every good relationship. If you want to be a colleague who is considered a valuable member, you must follow through with what you say you will do (ie, demonstrate integrity), which is an important precursor to trust. People simply will not trust someone who doesn't do what they say they will do. Once that integrity is established, people need to believe that you have their best interest in mind, or at the very least that you are not only out for your own interests. People simply will not trust colleagues who they suspect are only "in it" for themselves. To build trust, be a colleague who has other people's interests in mind and follow through with commitments.

Respect is another fundamental element to a friendly workplace. If you want to develop a quality professional relationship with your coworkers you must give them respect. Respect is a two-way street. In order to get respect, you must first give it—*first* being the operative word. Respect, in no uncertain terms, is admitting admiration for a colleague. The best way to show respect is conveying a sense of admiration for what someone has done. Developing good workplace relationships often hinges on one's willingness to show respect.

Being open-minded is another behavior that coworkers appreciate. This does not mean you have to accept or agree with everything that a colleague says or does, but it does mean you should be willing to listen and consider what they have to say and give them the benefit of the doubt in ambiguous or uncertain situations. Another aspect of being open-minded is to be alert to your own biases. Everyone has biases or defaults in their decision-making processes. Being aware of those is an important aspect of demonstrating open-mindedness.

Clear communication, the final characteristic, speaks for itself. If you want to develop good relationships with colleagues, try your best to articulate what you mean clearly and concisely. Beyond that, it is also important to, say what you mean and mean what you say;. While this sentiment is often indicative of integrity, it is also important for communication, being that the operative word is "say." Positive workplace relationships requires articulating clearly, usually beforehand, what is expected. Finally, be open, accessible, honest, and reciprocal in communication. These are the foundations needed to have a good relationship. Beyond these characteristics, there are specific action steps you can preform to establish yourself as a reliable and dependable colleague.

Workplace Behaviors That Matter

If you want to build better relationships at work, spend time developing your people skills. Many people have the misunderstanding that if they are an introvert or are task oriented, they get a free pass on developing interpersonal skills. Nothing could be further from the truth. Regardless of your personality, people skills are never optional. Developing people skills means practicing interpersonal communication, being willing to collaborate, and being committed to resolving conflicts as soon as they arise. Whether or not you are an introvert or extrovert, task oriented or people oriented, people skills matter. Learn to engage with people outside of required work contact.

Know that everyone needs contact beyond formal work contact. This is critical. People who have good relationships with their work colleagues schedule time to build relationships. Use small portions of your day, only a few minutes per day, to show you're friendly. Grab somebody a cup of coffee, help somebody replace office supplies, ask someone if you can pick up his or her mail since you're already going to the mailroom, etc. Limiting your contact with colleagues to only formal contact is detrimental to workplace morale.

Never hesitate to demonstrate gratitude toward coworkers. Good workplace relationships give way to compliments for a job well done. Don't be stingy with kind words—if someone has done something that is worthy of recognition, identify it. Other things people commonly do to establish good relationships with colleagues is to maintain and promote a positive attitude. It may be true that "misery loves company," but eventually it backfires. One of the best ways to maintain a positive relationship with colleagues is to stay positive and optimistic. People with good workplace relationships refuse to gossip. Perhaps nothing kills workplace relationships more quickly than gossip. Gossip fosters mistrust and animosity.

In summary, here is a list of the workplace behaviors we have discussed that work:

- Working on your people skills
- Addressing and resolving conflicts quickly
- Engaging with colleagues outside of required work activities
- Demonstrating gratitude
- Always looking for a positive spin
- Refusing to gossip

Discussion Questions

1. What are some of the key behaviors you need to develop to become a better colleague?
2. What are some of the threats in your workplace to good, collegial relationships?
3. What specific things can you do to improve your workplace reputation?
4. How would you describe the difference between your job satisfaction and your organizational commitment?

References

1. Saks AM. Antecedents and consequences of employee engagement. *Journal of Managerial Psychology.* 2006;21(7):600-619.
2. Andrew OC, Sofian S. Individual factors and work outcomes of employee engagement. *Procedia-Social and Behavioral Sciences.* 2012;40:498-508.
3. Building great relationships. MindTools Web site. https://www.mindtools.com/pages/article/good-relationships.htm. Accessed March 22, 2017.

QUESTION 13

Okay, I Was Asked to Lead a Team— How Do I Develop a Good Team That Performs Well?

One of the most common questions that health care professionals ask about leadership is how to develop a good team. We've already mentioned how diverse health care teams can be, and while that diversity is extremely valuable, it can be a source of tension—especially when trying to put together a high performing team. Michan and Rodger[1] performed a detailed literature review of teams within health care. They concluded that there are 3 overarching factors that must be addressed when developing a team. The first is organizational structure, followed by individual contribution, followed by clear team processes.

Developing a good team requires that the organization is structured to accommodate the work of the teams. If an organization's infrastructure, (eg, reward system, performance evaluations, bonuses) is geared to exploit and recognize individual performance above a team's performance, it might not have the appropriate structure. The first step in developing a good team is to review organizational structure. Organizational structures that accommodate team performance have a clear purpose for existence, have policies and procedures in place that recognize teamwork, delineate the tasks and roles of teams, provide adequate resources for teams, and ensure teams are led properly. Once organizational structure is set, it is necessary to explore how the individual's contribution contributes toward effective teamwork. To develop a good team, the individuals on that team must exhibit self-knowledge, display trust, show commitment, and demonstrate flexibility. Leaders must recruit and develop team members who are aware of their strengths and weaknesses, and not feel intimidated when someone else's strength is not their own. Team members must be willing to give trust before it is earned. Team commitment and expectations are delineated beforehand and should not be left to the individual to determine. Team members must demonstrate flexibility, especially when their project or agenda item is tabled for a more pressing issue. After the organization's structure is in place, and team members know how to contribute, team processes become important. Ironically, most people want to begin working on team processes immediately, when in fact they should come later in the team development cycle. The hard work, and perhaps even battle of developing good teams, is in establishing organizational structure and individual contribution; the easier part is team process. Team process includes establishing policy and procedure for team member's behaviors. Again, as counterintuitive as it might be, this should come last, and not first. Team processes should include rules (formal or informal) that address the following: team coordination and communication, decision-making processes, how to resolve and handle conflicts, how to resolve and handle social relationships, and how to conduct performance evaluations for team members.

To summarize, the team development process starts with exploring the organizational structure, which includes analyzing the organizations culture. This may require answering the question, is our organization structured to easily facilitate the input and work of teams? Another way to approach this question is to ask, does our organization's unwritten rules place a premium on team effort or individual effort? Developing a good team starts with acknowledging the reality of the organizational structure, and if necessary, collaborating with other individuals to change any undesirable aspects of the organizational structure. Once proper team structure is in place, you must turn your attention to the individual contribution of team members. Team members should be recruited based on their ability to work within teams. And finally, develop policies and procedures (formal processes) that govern the behavior of teams within the larger organization and between each other.

Kutz[2] identified team development stages within health care, which is a continuum of how teams evolve. Knowing these stages helps teams predict what to expect during development. The steps are confusion, dissatisfaction, resolution, and maturation. As a continuum, they do not have clear starting and ending points, but for the sake of explanation we will look at them in stages. Initially, teams encounter confusion. This confusion is usually precipitated by role ambiguity. It takes time for individual members of the team to become comfortable with their own role as well as the roles of other team members. Once roles are understood, there is usually a dissatisfaction that emerges, partly due to distrust of other team members and partly due to dissatisfaction in role assignment. These first 2 stages require frequent interaction and heavy input from a leader. The third stage is resolution. Once a team enters the resolution stage they become more self-governing, require less interaction (but that doesn't mean interaction decreases), and are more interdependent. Once they have some experience operating within the resolution stage, maturation occurs. Once a team achieves maturity, performance takes a dramatic uptick. This does not mean that a team cannot be performing well until this stage, only that once this stage is reached, performance increases dramatically and with much less effort. A mature team may take months or years to develop, but once it does it demonstrates several characteristics.

Nancarrow et al[3] conducted a thorough meta-analysis and identified several characteristics of effective (mature) health care teams, which include:

- Effective teams identify from within their ranks a leader who has a clear direction for the team. That leader in turn provides support to the other members.
- Effective teams incorporate agreed-upon values, and use these values to make decisions about team actions.
- Effective teams insist on trust, value everybody's contribution, and make decisions based on consensus (and not majority).
- Effective teams establish an infrastructure that supports their vision.
- Effective teams focus on documenting patient outcomes and utilize feedback to make improvements.
- Effective teams make collaborative decision-making a priority and communication occurs between the entire team, not just relevant parties.
- Effective teams assemble members who are best able (competent) to meet the needs of the patients.
- Effective teams recruit staff with interdisciplinary skills including cross functional abilities such as collaborative leadership, communication, professional knowledge, relevant experience, and team commitment.
- Effective teams are interdependent, but respectful of individual roles and abilities.
- Effective teams encourage personal development of team members.

Discussion Questions

1. Consider one of the teams you participate on; what stage of development are you currently in?
2. Is the organizational structure of your organization conducive to building effective teams?
3. Considering the individual contributions of team members, what are your weaknesses and what are your strengths?
4. What team processes need to be established on your teams to expedite efficiency?
5. What is one of the major obstacles you see as prohibiting the effective development of teams within your organization?
6. What is one of the major facilitators within your organization that assists with developing effective teams?

References

1. Michan S, Rodger S. Characteristics of effective teams: a literature review. *Aust Health Rev.* 2000;23(3):201-208.
2. Kutz MR. *Leadership and Management in Athletic Training: An Integrated Approach.* Philadelphia, PA: Lippincott Williams & Wilkins; 2010.
3. Nancarrow SA, Booth A, Ariss S, Smith T, Enderby P, Roots A. Ten principles of good interdisciplinary team work. *Hum Resour Health.* 2013;11(1):19.

QUESTION 14

Why Is It so Hard to Communicate Clearly on Teams Made Up of a Variety of Different Professionals?

Communication can be volatile. It is generally accepted that communication is a good thing, and it is, but what qualifies as "good communication" is different for different people. Not only are there major communication differences between the sexes—just look at any relationship section in your local bookstore—but there are also huge differences in communication preferences between other demographic characteristics (eg, education level, ethnicity, culture, experience). Despite these differences, when teams communicate things generally improve. So, how does one communicate effectively on teams, especially on diverse teams? Part of the answer can be found in understanding the difference between high-context and low-context cultures.

Communicating in Diverse Contexts (High Versus Low Context)

Communicating within diverse teams can be difficult, especially if that diversity is based in cultural or ethnic expectations. The difficulty is exacerbated when different cultures have embedded or intrinsic differences within their communication styles. Many of the differences between cultures can be described as high-context or low-context.[1] Basically, high-context communication is when the communicator assumes everyone else (eg, listeners) knows what he or she means and therefore fails to be clear, concise, and explicit, so a lot is left to the imagination or memory of the listener. High-context communicators assume that others perceive the same things that they do. High-context cultures (Mediterranean, Slavic, Central European, Latin American, African, Arab, Asian, Native American) leave much of the message unspecified.[2] In high-context cultures, openly disagreeing with someone in public is insulting.[1] On the other hand, low-context communication is when the communicator assumes nothing about what the listener hears and is very explicit. Low-context cultures (most Germanic and English-speaking countries) expect messages to be obvious and specific.[2] In a low-context message, information is explicit and nothing is left to the imagination.[1] There are pros and cons with both types. High-context communicators give the benefit of the doubt, but can often fall into the trap of presuming that everyone else knows what they mean. Low-context communicators are clear and explicit, but can fall into the trap of appearing to be condescending.

TABLE 14-1	
HIGH- AND LOW-CONTEXT COMMUNICATION STYLE PREFERENCES	
HIGH-CONTEXT COMMUNICATION	**LOW-CONTEXT COMMUNICATION**
Indirect and implicit messages	Direct, simple, and clear messages
High use of nonverbal communication	Low use of nonverbal communication
Low reliance on written communication	High reliance on written communication
Use intuition and feelings to make decisions	Reliance on facts and evidence for decisions
Relationships are more important than schedules	Schedules are more important than relationships
Adapted from Maclachlan M. Cross-Cultural communication styles: high and low context. Communicaid Web Site. https://www.communicaid.com/cross-cultural-training/blog/high-and-low-context/. Published February 12, 2010. Accessed July 28, 2017.	

Being that so many health care teams have a high level of cultural and ethnic diversity, understanding the nuances of high- and low-context preferences can be extremely helpful. Failing to understand these nuances may contribute significantly to workplace frustration. Therefore, part of the difficulty with communicating on a diverse team is not understanding the nuances of high- and low-context communication styles. While much of the literature on high- and low-context communication centers on different cultures, it is not exclusive to cultures. Differences between high- and low-context communication is also a significant source of workplace conflict regardless of culture.

Table 14-1 shows some general preferences of people with high- and low-context communication styles.[3]

Discussion Questions

1. Are you a high-context or low-context communicator?
2. What are some strategies you can implement to better understand the other communication preference?
3. What is the communication preference of the person you often have the most conflict with?
4. How have you considered your coworkers perspective relative to difficulty communicating with you?
5. What can you do so that your coworkers can better understand what you are trying to communicate?

References

1. Hall ET. *Beyond Culture*. New York, NY: Random House; 1976.
2. Goman C. Communicating Across Cultures. American Society of Mechanical Engineers Web site. https://www.asme.org/engineering-topics/articles/business-communication/communicating-across-cultures. Published March, 2011. Accessed July 28, 2017.
3. Maclachlan M. Cross-Cultural communication styles: high and low context. Communicaid Web Site. https://www.communicaid.com/cross-cultural-training/blog/high-and-low-context/. Published February 12, 2010. Accessed July 28, 2017.

QUESTION 15

Is There Something I Can Do Better to Communicate Well With All the Members of My Team?

In the last chapter, we discussed why it is difficult to communicate clearly when teams are diverse. In this chapter, we will address specific strategies that can be implemented to increase the effectiveness of our communication, especially when teams are diverse.

Communication takes place between 2 or more parties, the communicator (ie, the person sending the message) and the receiver (ie, the person receiving the message). Both parties have an obligation to the communication process. In every communication exchange there is a perceptual screen. The perceptual screen is the lens through which one interacts with others, and it influences the quality, accuracy, and clarity of the communication.[1]

Daft and Lengel[2] identify several ways in which a person communicates (eg, face-to-face, telephone, email), and the information richness and data capacity of each way. Information richness is the meaning and emotion associated with the content; and data capacity is the uninterrupted and unanalyzed material. For example, face-to-face discussion has a very high information richness, but a very low data capacity. On the other hand, a formal written report has low information richness, but high data capacity. Telephone is similar to face-to-face, and email is moderate in both categories. The idea being that it is important to know the strengths and weaknesses of the mode of communication you are using. For emotionally charged content, face-to-face discussion is much better, for everyday normal and routine communication email is sufficient, and for conveying high volumes of information with little emotional connection, a written report is appropriate. Defaulting to one way all or most of the time is poor communication. To be effective, it is critical that you understand the strengths and weaknesses of the different ways in which you send messages. Be proactive and use face-to-face discussion when information richness is needed and email only when data is high and information richness is not necessary.

Aspects of Active Listening

Active (or reflective) listening is one of the most important behaviors of good communicators. However, reflective listening also has glaring and obvious weaknesses. In fact, contemporary research is beginning to show it is less effective than most people generally think it is, especially during conflict.[3,4] Despite its weaknesses, reflective listening is still recommended. Reflective listening is the purposeful interaction with the sender of the message, which includes repeating back to the speaker what you believe they want you to know. In addition to repeating back this information, it is also appropriate to add affirming contact. Affirming contact is periodically saying during the course of the conversation "I see," "okay," or "yes, I understand." It is also appropriate to paraphrase what is being expressed. This means periodically interjecting during the course of the conversation with what you think you just heard. Clarify the implicit—meaning, when you sense that an idea is not being accurately or fully expressed, ask the sender of the message to pause and rephrase what it is you think you just heard. Reflect back what you think the core feelings are of the person who is sending the message. Reflective listeners also practice silence. This does not mean a prolonged or exaggerated span of silence, just enough silence so that the communicator can convey his or her entire thought. It should go without saying, but eye contact is imperative. Finally, reflective listeners engage in two-way communication instead of one-way communication. This means allowing time and space for both parties to be heard. In summary, the reflective listener does the following things:

- Repeats back to the speaker the main point they believe they want them to hear
- Gives affirming contact
- Paraphrases expressed ideas
- Clarifies implicit ideas
- Reflects core feelings back
- Practices the right amount of silence
- Maintains eye contact
- Promotes two-way communication

By practicing reflective listening, teams stand a much better chance of resolving, or even avoiding misunderstandings and miscommunication. However, as mentioned earlier, there are weaknesses to reflective listening. The most obvious being during conflict. When in conflict, it may not be helpful to reflect back to the listener exactly what it is that they want you to do, especially when the best remedy is behavioral. For example, Gottman and Silver[4] cite an example of 2 people in conflict over failing to perform an agreed-upon duty. It does little good for the guilty party to repeat back to them why they are upset if the neglected duty is still never performed. In summary, be sure that the medium you use to convey information is appropriate for the type of information you are trying to convey and be sure to engage in and practice reflective listening techniques. These 2 strategies can be very helpful in avoiding communication misunderstandings.

Discussion Questions

1. What do you believe are the differences that teammates assume contribute to communication misunderstandings?
2. Why do you believe it is easier to text or email information-rich content instead of having face-to-face dialogue?
3. What is something you can do to enhance your skills and ability to convey information-rich content in face-to-face communications?
4. What are 3 areas of reflective communication in which you need to develop?
5. What aspect of reflective listening do you believe you are good at? Would the people who know you well agree?

References

1. Nelson DL, Quick JC. *ORGB: Organizational Behavior*. Boston, MA: Cengage Learning; 2015.
2. Daft RL, Lengel RH. Information richness: a new approach to managerial behavior and organizational design. *Research in Organizational Behavior*. 1984;6:191-233.
3. Weisinger H, Pawliw-Fry JP. *Performing Under Pressure: The Science of Doing Your Best When it Matters Most*. New York, NY: Crown Business; 2015.
4. Gottman J, Silver N. *The Seven Principles for Making Marriage Work: A Practical Guide From the Country's Foremost Relationship Expert*. New York, NY: Three Rivers Press; 1999.

QUESTION 16

Shouldn't They Just Do What I Say? Why Do I Need to Communicate Clearly? Everyone Knows We Have a Job to Do.

This question may seem obvious, but unfortunately many people give up trying to communicate clearly too soon. Yes, it is uncommon to find someone who does not believe that clear communication is important. Furthermore, few people would argue over the value of clear communication. However, staying the course and consistently giving an effort to communicate clearly is difficult. It is becoming more common to find coworkers who have given up on trying to communicate clearly. People give up trying to communicate clearly when they perceive others simply will not or do not listen. However, failures in communication, especially within health care, can be extremely expensive both fiscally and for morale.[1]

Unfortunately, during prolonged conflict or hostility, too many people neglect the fact that communication is a two-way street. By that, I mean when there is a communication breakdown it often involves deficiencies from both parties. One of the key steps that can help ensure clear communication is to take inventory of your own communication styles and techniques. Be sure that you are communicating in the most appropriate way possible and do not take your own word for it, ask others for input. However rare, there are times when the environment is hostile and no amount of effort seems to help. In these situations, should teams continue to work towards clear communication in the workplace? Yes.

Benefits of Good Communication

When clinicians engage in clear and open communication with patients, clinical outcomes (both physiological and psychological) improve dramatically.[2,3] There is also evidence to suggest that when team members communicate clearly with each other, patient outcomes also improve. Clear communication shows *esprit de corps* among members of the health care team, helps to avoid expensive medical errors, and simplifies patient care by preventing delays.[4] A grounded-theory study found that when nurses communicate effectively with each other, patient outcomes are improved.[5] Manser[6] was able to show that good communication does contribute towards better teamwork, which is directly tied to improved patient outcomes. Schmalenberg and Kramer[4] also reported improved outcomes when physicians and nurses communicated clearly with each other. There does seem to be evidence to indicate that clear communication, although the mechanisms are unknown, contributes towards improved patient outcomes. Therefore, every effort must be made to communicate clearly not only with patients, but also with coworkers.

Within health care, there is often tension between wanting to say what one truly thinks and feels but doesn't for fear of offending someone. I've heard it expressed this way, "I want to be a good communicator, but being a good communicator gets me in trouble." You may have experienced this sentiment, but implicit in that statement is that good communication is being able to say anything to anybody. That is where the mistake is made. It has always been wise to avoid saying anything and everything that immediately comes to mind.

Kreps and Kunimoto[7] use an iceberg analogy for the issues within communication. They identify race, gender, age, and nationality as the piece of the iceberg that everybody sees floating above the water. Obviously, these factors need to be taken into consideration when communicating with team members. Beneath the surface of the water (what cannot be seen but has a large impact on communication) are, among other things, socioeconomic status, occupation, health condition, religion, group membership, education, and politics. These "out of sight" issues are also important and should be taken into consideration when communicating with team members. If these out of sight issues are given full consideration, it is safe to assume communication will be better. Therefore, when communicating sensitive issues or issues pertinent to patient safety, it is critical that the sender of the message be cognizant of the message they are sending despite the words. Likewise, the receiver of the message must be attuned to his or her own attitude and biases, which will help mitigate any confusion.

Communicating Clearly

Handling communication requires extreme sensitivity. The best way to practice that level of sensitivity is to be above reproach in your communication. Always, be honest, forthright, and genuine. This is not an oversimplification. It can be best demonstrated by simply considering the other person's feelings and point of view; and living by the mantra, *if you don't know, don't assume.* Communicating effectively means being clear and concise. One of the major obstacles in this arena is around the use of metaphor and colloquialisms. I have spent a significant amount of time in other countries, and one of the biggest mistakes I have made in failing to communicate with colleagues tended to be in assuming that other people would automatically know what I meant (this is what I referred to in a previous chapter as high-context communication). The fact is, often times, metaphors and colloquialisms are lost. Therefore, good communicators need to reframe everything for the benefit of the listener. To do that takes time, but the reward is worth it.

The second obstacle is the risk of offense. Most people, especially in a professional and fast-paced context like health care, are not purposely trying to offend. Most of the time, offense that takes place is quickly identified, rectified, and forgiven. Therefore, we are not addressing here discrimination or antagonistic behavior. However, there are times when a simple misunderstanding is taken offensively. The best way to avoid these types of situations is to not make assumptions about someone else's frame of mind, values, experience, or beliefs. It is best to give the benefit of the doubt and when communication is suspect, ask nonthreatening or nonaccusatory clarifying questions about what was meant or implied. Never assume you know what was implied. What seems like an obvious implication to you often times never even occurred to the other party— because you also are filtering what you hear through your own biases, something of which they may know nothing about. Remember at all times miscommunication and failure to understand is always a two-way street. Own your part of any miscommunication and learn from those times. In the end, if we can take time to communicate clearly, morale is increased and patients experience improved outcomes.

Discussion Questions

1. Think of a time when you assumed somebody meant something other than what they did—when did you realize it and how did you rectify it?

2. How does the fast pace of a modern health care facility contribute toward communication dysfunction?

3. What can you do personally within a fast-paced health care facility to minimize communication breakdown?

4. What would you recommend to your department or organization to facilitate clear communication between colleagues?

5. How have you experienced clear communication between clinicians directly benefiting patients?

References

1. Calloway S. Preventing communication breakdowns. *Rn.* 2001;64(1):71-83.

2. Stewart MA. Effective physician-patient communication and health outcomes: a review. *Can Med Assoc J.* 1995;152(9):1423.

3. Street RL, Makoul G, Arora NK, Epstein RM. How does communication heal? Pathways linking clinician-patient communication to health outcomes. *Patient Educ and Couns.* 2009;74(3).295-301.

4. Schmalenberg C, Kramer M. Nurse-physician relationships in hospitals: 20,000 nurses tell their story. *Crit Care Nurse.* 2009;29(1):74-83.

5. Propp KM, Apker J, Zabava Ford WS, Wallace N, Serbenski M, Hofmeister N. Meeting the complex needs of the health care team: identification of nurse—team communication practices perceived to enhance patient outcomes. *Qual Health Res.* 2010;20(1):15-28.

6. Manser T. Teamwork and patient safety in dynamic domains of healthcare: a review of the literature. *Acta Anaesthesiol Scand.* 2009;53(2):143-151.

7. Kreps GL, Kunimoto EN. *Effective Communication in Multicultural Health Care Settings, Vol. 3.* Thousand Oaks, CA: Sage Publications; 1994.

QUESTION 17

What Is Followership, and How Is It Possibly Related to Leadership?

Followers define leadership. Therefore, the real power in an organization rests with followers. Followership is a growing phenomenon within the leadership and management literature. It is generally understood that there is no leadership without followers, yet followers are often left out of the leadership equation.[1] Leadership is a process that is cocreated in social and relational interactions between people.[2] As a cocreated social interaction, followers contribute an incredibly important feature to the leadership dynamic. Stated simply, without followers there is no leadership. Figure 17-1 is a simple illustration of this process. Note that it is the follower's paradigm, or follower's perceptions, that give meaning to leadership. A leader acts, the follower interprets those actions respective to his or her understanding of the context, and leadership is then determined to be effective or noneffective. Since a leader cannot define or determine their own outcomes, it is left to the follower and the context to assign meaning to the leader's actions. This places an incredible amount of responsibility and power on the follower in the follower's ability to diagnose and understand the context.

Failure to consider yourself a follower and failure to develop your followership can have a negative impact on your organization and your own leadership. It is difficult, maybe impossible, to be a good leader without also being a good follower. Regardless of your position or rank, being a good follower requires a willingness to defer to someone else. Simply put, this means allowing yourself to be influenced. In fact, some believe by allowing yourself to be influenced you are in fact putting yourself in the position of power. Chester Barnard[3] describes this phenomenon relative to the concept of submission (eg, followership) as an essential behavior benefiting both the leader and the follower. He claimed the determination of authority always lies with the follower, and described submission, or deference as Fairhurst and Uhl-Bien[2] put it, as the voluntary yielding of control to another. Later, Meindl[4] picked up on this idea and stated that leadership is in the eye of the beholder; therefore, followers define what it is and how it looks—not leaders. Thus, followers experience a twofold benefit within the leadership dynamic of being able to confer authority to an individual, as well as empower themselves. Consequently, followership is a powerful leadership behavior that cannot be ignored.

Ironically, despite all the attention given to leaders and leadership, it is far more common to find followers within an organization. Numerically within any organization there are simply more followers than leaders. Therefore, it is incumbent upon any legitimate leadership development to

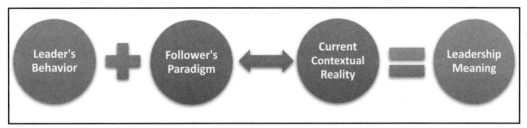

Figure 17-1. Follower's role in leadership meaning.

give attention to followership development, which indirectly enhances an organization's capacity to lead and accomplish goals. Furthermore, it is highly likely that over the course of one's career, or within even the course of a single day, a person will be both leader and follower.[5] It has been said that followers who are familiar with leadership, who can recognize a leader's flawed thinking, and appropriately challenge that thinking, have a tremendous value to today's organizations.[6] Proactive followership is essential for good leadership, morale, and organizational success.

Taking that into consideration, it is important to ask what are the attributes of a good follower? Attributes of a good follower include the following characteristics:

- Raises difficult and challenging issues that leaders are unaware of or ignore
- Understands the construct of leadership and how it works within an organization
- Is familiar with the different leadership styles of those formal positions of authority
- Is aware of the written and unwritten rules that influence behavior
- Willingly defers to others
- Has concerns for others
- Advocates for others and different ideas
- Intentionally contributes to the overall process and goals
- Disagrees privately, but supports publicly
- Refuses to throw colleagues or supervisors "under the bus"

Discussion Questions

1. In your opinion, who is a role model follower you can refer to as a mentor? What makes them a good follower?
2. How have you seen followership benefit your organization or department?
3. What would you say to colleagues to encourage them to be better followers?
4. Can you describe how good followership can be of benefit to an organization?
5. Can you describe how you believe followership is different from compliance?

References

1. Uhl-Bien M, Riggio RE, Lowe KB, Carsten MK. Followership theory: a review and research agenda. *Leadersh Q.* 2014;25(1):83-104.
2. Fairhurst GT, Uhl-Bien M. Organizational discourse analysis (ODA): Examining leadership as a relational process. *Leadersh Q.* 2012;23(6):1043–1062.
3. Barnard CI. *The Functions of the Executive.* Cambridge, MA: Harvard University Press; 1968.
4. Meindl JR. The romance of leadership as a follower-centric theory: a social constructionist approach. *Leadersh Q.* 1995;6(3):329-341.
5. Crossman B, Crossman J. Conceptualizing followership—a review of the literature. *Leadership.* 2011;7(4):481-497.
6. Carsten MK, Uhl-Bien M, West BJ, Patera JL, McGregor R. Exploring social constructions of followership: a qualitative study. *Leadersh Q.* 2011;21:543-562.

SECTION IV

QUESTIONS ABOUT CHANGE

QUESTION 18

Everyone Talks About Change Like It Is the Plague—Why Is Change so Difficult?

Health care is all about change. Within health care, one of the most requested attributes of leaders is the ability to bring about change.[1] If you want to be involved in health care, regardless of the discipline, you must learn to accept and embrace change.

Change in its most simple form is an alteration or modification. A song comes on the radio we don't like, we change the station; there is an obstacle in our path, we change directions; we spill something on our shirt, we change shirts; our patient's treatment isn't working, we change treatments. All of these changes we do routinely, without much thought, and with very little stress. The reality is, change is something we do every day, do it well, and do it automatically. Despite this, people often experience change as a threat and compensate for it by defaulting to well-learned and familiar behaviors.[2] Ironically, these default behaviors, which we worked so hard to learn, sabotage our ability to change and grow. This is partly why evidence-based practice and continuing education requirements are so important. Without these to challenge our clinical decisions we might fall into unchallenged routines. To overcome these defaults we must consistently and constantly engage in unfamiliar and challenging behaviors.[3]

Despite the usefulness of change, it is likely that you have heard someone say, "if it ain't broke don't fix it," or "don't change for the sake of change." Ironically, these sentiments violate what we know to be true from biology and physics. These sentiments are rooted in fear, not reality. The very essence of biological systems are based on change, both gradual and rapid. In physics, we know that when something is left to itself it will eventually wear down and break—this is the law of entropy. Change is a basic scientific necessity of complex systems, and to fight it or resist it is futile and a waste of valuable energy.

Since change is essential, it makes sense to try and understand why we resist it and how we can become better at it. We resist change because it threatens our sense of control and disrupts the status quo. Change is easy, like changing the radio dial, as long as the decision to change it is ours. However, think about your reaction when someone else changes your radio dial. Your initial response is most likely, "keep your hands off my dial." How ironic for such a nonconsequential action. Now, make it a consequential action like something related to your livelihood and our

Kutz MR. *Leadership Questions for Health Care Professionals:*
Applying Theories & Principles to Practice (pp 65-75).
© 2018 SLACK Incorporated.

reaction can be self-sabotaging. The concept of change is disconcerting because we believe we have lost control, and without that control we think, usually contrary to probability, that things will get worse. The reality is that most of the time change ends up making us better. But, because it is unknown we think it is safer to assume the worst, and consequently, sabotage the change process. In summary, we dislike change because of the fear of the unknown and a perceived loss of our sense of control. What are some behaviors we can practice to make the change easier to handle? Here are some basic tips you can practice to help you handle change more effectively:

- Accept the fact that change is essential to growth.
- Work to maintain an optimistic perspective.
- Stay connected to colleagues and coworkers.
- Frequently take time to self-reflect.
- Learn new skills and do new things (both personally and professionally).
- Ask more questions.
- Think differently—welcome change as an opportunity to learn about yourself.

Discussion Questions

1. What are your default behavior(s)/attitude(s) to *unexpected* change?
2. What is your general feeling and reaction to *anticipated* change?
3. Recall a recent change. What was the perspective of the people around you relative to that change? What were the similarities, and what were the differences?
4. How do you handle change that is brought on by someone else?
5. If you could single-handedly make one change in your organization or department, what would it be? How do you believe that change would affect others?
6. Think of a change initiative you are currently engaged in (or that you know is coming). Practice articulating the big picture outcomes of this change and the smaller, less significant, corollary changes that might be associated with this change.

References

1. Dye CF. *Leadership in Healthcare: Essential Values and Skills.* 3rd ed. Chicago, IL: Health Administration Press; 2017.
2. Nelson DL, Quick JC. *ORGB5: Organizational Behavior.* Boston, MA: Cengage; 2016.
3. Kutz M. *Contextual Intelligence: How Thinking in 3D Can Help Resolve Complexity, Uncertainty and Ambiguity.* New York, NY: Springer Press; 2017.

QUESTION 19

People Seem to Dislike Change, but Embrace Innovation—What Is the Difference Between Change and Innovation?

In Question 18, we answered why change is difficult. In this response, we will address innovation and how it is different from change. As we described in the last question, change is an alteration or modification to something that currently exists. As such, change is rooted in the past, in that it never fully emancipates its central tenet. Innovation, on the other hand, is rooted in the future and it completely jettisons any former tenet. Innovation is a brand new idea or product, or a brand new use for an existing product. Innovation comes from the Latin root *novus*, which means novel or new. To *innovate* is to introduce something brand-new (as opposed to modify something existing) or alter something so dramatically that it is completely different from an established practice. Ironically, people typically get excited about innovation (compared to being nervous or skeptical about change).

Innovation is considered to be a critical component of productivity and competitive survival.[1] Without innovation it is impossible to remain sustainable. Health care institutions are facing an increasing need for innovation in order to become competitive and offer new treatments for patients.[2] There is a general consensus that an intentional absence of innovation is conceding defeat. Therefore, exploring the causes of innovation, especially within health care is essential, so that leaders can look for opportunities to introduce innovation in their professions, organizations, and departments.

Drivers of Innovation

Peter Drucker[3], perhaps the world's foremost expert on innovation, identified 7 drivers of innovation. These drivers of innovation are the sources behind what makes innovation necessary. Occurring within an industry or organization, like health care, are 4 of the drivers—3 of the drivers are external or independent of an industry or organization, yet still have a profound impact on specific industries.

The first 4 drivers of innovation (those drivers that are present within an industry, such as health care) are:

1. **The unexpected:** The enemy of the status quo is the unexpected. In reality, when something happens that is unexpected, people (leaders and followers) stop and take notice. It is the very act of taking notice the sparks new ideas. Unfortunately when things are going well, people rarely stop to take notice. According to Drucker,[3] unexpected success is one of the best drivers for innovation. It is also important to recognize unexpected failure or an unexpected outside event also contributes to innovation. When we can train our health care workers to anticipate the unexpected there is a better chance for innovation.

2. **Incongruity:** All too often there is a discrepancy between what one thinks "should" happen and what actually happens (should they take the time to find out what actually happens). This can be best illustrated with the equation 1+1=3; obviously this is not possible in mathematics, but in real life, it is plausible that 2 things do not add up to what they should. An incongruity occurs when things don't add up as they are supposed to. Relative to innovation, this is a good thing. This can be an incredible source for innovation because most people assume incorrectly about what is supposed to be, which forces rethinking problems and solutions.

3. **Process need:** There is an old proverb that says, "Necessity is the mother of invention." Process need serves to perfect a process that already exists. Think of replacing the weakest link in a chain or redesigning a former policy around new information. Process need drives innovation by examining existing practices that already work in an attempt to make them work better. The irony of course is examining, with the intent to modify, something that is already working, which most people do not do.

4. **Changes in industry structure:** This is when something within an industry changes dramatically, which forces everyone else to reinvent how they currently do business. An example of this in health care is the advent of electronic medical records and its impact on health care.

The second set of drivers occur outside of a specific industry, but are present within a larger culture or community. They are:

5. **Changes in demographics:** Nothing tricky here. The example is a change in population or the needs of a particular demographic. According to Drucker,[3] this is described as any change in population relative to size, age distribution, composition, ethnic status, employment, educational status, or income. One example of this within health care that is driving many innovative ideas is the aging of the baby boomer population and the expectations of millennials.

6. **Changes in perception, mood, and meaning:** Over time things tend to shift. Keeping up with those shifts is not always a priority, especially if things are going well. Unfortunately, failing to keep up with those shifts typically requires a dramatic innovation once someone realizes that things have shifted beyond his or her capacity. An example is how social media has changed the operational definition of friend. These new ideas often drive creative and innovative ideas.

7. **New knowledge:** Drucker[3] states that knowledge-based innovation is the superstar of industrialized society. New knowledge in this case means exactly what it sounds like. When something new is discovered, typically technologically-based (but it is not limited to technology)—a good example of this is what research can generate—innovation is required. New knowledge is the idea behind evidence-based practice. Presumably, clinical decisions are based on the best available clinical evidence, which presumably is ongoing. Therefore, this new knowledge should drive new behaviors.

Each of the 7 drivers of innovation contribute considerable force in the creation of new and needed products and ideas. This is important in health care because new products and ideas are central for staying competitive and offering the highest quality and most cost-effective patient care. Any of the 7 drivers can be active at any time and may even overlap with each other. When they do, it makes innovation even more necessary. Ignoring the 7 drivers is to concede defeat. Leaders, especially those in a complex and dynamic environment like health care, must be constantly looking for the 7 drivers, which can serve as a major impetus to promote innovation. It is important to remember that innovation, and not change, is more likely to have a positive and profound impact on outcomes. Consequently, it is incumbent upon health care professionals, regardless of the discipline, to think in terms of innovation instead of change.

Discussion Questions

1. Why do you think most people typically embrace innovation but fear change?
2. In your opinion, does health care need change or innovation?
3. In your own words, how would you describe the difference between *the unexpected* and an *incongruity*?
4. How does your organization or profession respond to change vs innovation?
5. Which of the 7 drivers is the most common source of innovation within your specific health care setting or occupation?
6. What innovation needs to happen within health care or your profession?
7. What do you need to do to be more innovative?
8. Which one of the 7 drivers of innovation is the most appealing to you? Why?

References

1. Omachonu VK, Einspruch NG. Innovation in healthcare delivery systems: a conceptual framework. *Innov J.* 2010;15(1):1-20.
2. Moreira MR, Gherman M, Sousa PS. Does innovation influence the performance of healthcare organizations? *Innovation.* 2017;19(3):335-352.
3. Drucker P. *Innovation and Entrepreneurship.* New York, NY: Routledge; 2015.

QUESTION 20

I Need to Get a New Change Initiated—Is There a Best or Better Way to Do That?

In the last 2 questions, we discussed why change is difficult and how change is different from innovation. In this question, I would like to discuss best practice strategies for implementing change. A common question among health care professionals is, how can I get the people around me or the organization I am in to change? Admittedly, this is not always easy, but there are some behaviors that you can do to help facilitate the process of initiating change.

Once the fear of change has been overcome, initiating it can still be difficult. Typically, one or more of the following barriers are present when it comes time to initiating change:

- Lack of support from those in authority
- Resistance or skepticism from others
- Hesitancy to invest resources in something "unproven"
- Shortage of resources
- Influence of ambiguity
- Over-reliance on willpower
- Failing to realize that doing nothing (or waiting) is doing something

Fortunately, it is possible to overcome these barriers. John Kotter, Harvard Professor and perhaps the world's foremost expert on the process of change, has identified an 8-step process for initiating change, despite barriers. Kotter's[1] 8-step change process includes the following:

1. **Establish a sense of urgency:** One of the keys to this step is battling complacency. As we have stated previously, the status quo is one of the largest obstacles to forward movement of any kind. As Kotter indicated in this first step, establishing a sense of urgency combats complacency. It is paramount that leaders increase urgency. In fact, Kotter even goes so far as to suggest it may be necessary for a leader to create a crisis. The idea being that few things get people's attention like a good old-fashioned crisis. Another way to increase urgency is utilize the strengths, weaknesses, opportunities, and threat (SWOT) analysis by ensuring awareness

of weaknesses and highlighting external threats. This may seem counterintuitive, especially pointing out weaknesses, but this does not mean to belittle anyone. Ideally, these are weaknesses they have identified themselves already. Once identified, insist that performance evaluations are realistic and honest. Keeping everyone abreast of the external threats to their current practice also increases urgency.

2. **Create a guided coalition:** It is dangerous to believe that change is the sole responsibility of a single charismatic leader. Once a sense of urgency is established, it is important to develop a team who understands the urgency and is committed to making change happen. The critical element for this step is to be sure that the right people are on the team, which can take time. Change teams need the proper balance of expertise and influence. Experts alone are not enough, and influencers alone are not enough. To create buy-in, team members must be both influential and expert.

3. **Develop a vision and strategy:** Ironically, most leaders try to initiate change by micromanaging individual behaviors or outright authoritarian decrees. Needless to say, those efforts are usually futile. Developing a vision and strategy requires painting a desirable picture of the future. Leaders often fail to let followers know the intended outcome—in the long term—of the desired change. Effective change strategists make appeals based on a desirable future, one which they have taken time to describe to others. An effective vision is usually imaginable, desirable, feasible, flexible, and able to be communicated easily.

4. **Communicate the change vision:** A great vision is worthless unless it is able to be communicated clearly. It is essential that change initiatives and their desired outcome be clearly communicated. Some of the fundamental aspects of clearly communicating change is that the change is simple, is clear of all jargon and technobabble, high in metaphor and analogy, repeated often, modeled by example, and is open for dialogue.

5. **Empower others for action:** Empowering others for action means giving people the necessary resources they need to make something happen. These resources are not only financial, but also personal, structural, and emotional. One of the biggest obstacles to empowering employees to make the changes that are necessary is existing structure. Often times, our organization's structure prevents change. The degree of empowerment necessary for dramatic change must go beyond giving people permission, it includes permission, but it also must include emotional and financial support, and structural alignment that facilitates easy change.

6. **Generate short-term wins:** The big picture is important, but people must see that they are making strides towards the ultimate goal. Nothing kills momentum more than failing to recognize forward progress. It is important to design short-term wins into the overall change process. When short-term wins are present, they provide evidence that sacrifice is worth it, it rewards change agents with the proverbial "pat on the back," it helps find big picture vision items, silences critics, and keeps people's momentum.

7. **Consolidate gains:** When short-term gains are seen, additional gains are more likely. Steps 1 through 6 influence how change is perceived. Once you get to this point, change is starting to become appreciated and even expected. The interesting part here is that now people are looking for other changes that need to be made that will add to the overall vision. Once this begins to happen, it is important to leverage additional help by recruiting more members to the change coalition. There will always be those who are skeptical, but by this point some of those skeptics will be able to be swayed, especially if you remain patient with them. Ultimately, consolidating gains is about identifying additional change in continuing to move forward.

8. **Anchor new approaches in the culture:** Finally, the last step in Kotter's 8-step change process involves having a culture. Once change becomes the status quo, you have to work to maintain it. The work requires keeping the positive outcomes of change visible.

Kotter's 8 steps cannot occur overnight. It should not be assumed that this is a simple, quick, or easy 8-step process. The type of change being suggested ultimately results in a fundamental shift in the culture of an industry or organization. Consequently, it takes time. In fact, Michael Fullan,[2] noted change expert, states that developing a culture of change involves slow learning over time. Short-term wins (step 6) should always be part of a larger change initiative, which may be more immediate. However, it is important not to sacrifice the more immediate for the big picture. In summary, change and innovation are both critical to survival. To introduce incremental change is to understand that it is incremental. Consistency is the key to ultimately arriving at the needed change.

Discussion Questions

1. Think of an example when one of the barriers to change negatively impacted morale in your workplace. How could it have been handled differently?

2. What could you do more effectively to help make needed changes happen?

3. If you were to be asked to launch a new change initiative in your department, how would you go about implementing step 1 (creating a sense of urgency)? Be specific.

4. Take an inventory of your current key members within your organization. Which ones would you want to be on your change coalition team? Why? (What attitudes or behaviors do they bring that you need?)

5. Considering your response to question 4—of the people not on your change team, what could you do to begin to sway them to become a valuable member?

6. Identify a specific change initiative needed in your workplace. How would you communicate the importance of a change initiative vision-like statement?

References

1.   Kotter JP. *Leading Change*. Boston, MA: Harvard Business Review Press; 2012.
2.   Fullan M. *Leading in a Culture of Change Personal Action Guide and Workbook*. Hoboken, NJ: John Wiley & Sons; 2004.

QUESTION 21

Is Work-Life Balance a Real Thing? How Can I Balance Them, and Will That Balance Reduce Burnout?

Burnout affects many health care clinicians and ultimately contributes toward many clinicians leaving health care. Burnout is a long-term stress reaction, which includes emotional exhaustion, depersonalization, and a lack of sense of personal accomplishment.[1] Linzer and colleagues[1] also identified several factors that contribute toward burnout of health care professionals, including:

- Time pressures in the office/clinic
- Frenzied work environment
- Ineffective teamwork
- Personal and workplace values not aligning
- Lack of control over work
- Implementing electronic medical records
- Poor work-life interface

Implementing work-life balance strategies may help to combat the onset of burnout and enhance overall morale. Ironically, and despite its strong presence in the literature, a single agreed upon definition of work-life balance has remained uncharacteristically elusive.[2] Suffice it to say, most people understand it to imply time off (or time away from the office) to pursue interests outside of work, and includes having a level of control over how much time one spends at work.

An emerging question in contemporary organizational research asks, is there such a thing as work-life balance? The question has meaning because there seems to be a presumption that it is not possible for "life" to provide meaning and value to work, or that one's work does not add value and meaning to life. It is as if our culture forces this dichotomy, which may not have historical precedent. In many cultures around the world, work adds value to life and vice versa. The 2 do not need to be understood to be mutually exclusive.

Some propose that work-life balance, based on a concept of 50/50, is not possible and short-sighted (ie, 50% of joy and meaning come from work, and 50% comes from nonwork activities). Work-life balance is not about equal time spent in either area[3]—it is about having the option to engage in different activities that provide meaning. Work should be one of those activities that provide meaning, but certainly not the only activity. If balance is not 50/50, it might help to look at balance from a different perspective. In my experience, a more accurate description of work-life alance is a series of "alternating" 90/10, and that the more correct term is work-life *integration*. Alternating 90/10's requires a long-term view and implies that there are times and seasons of life when 90% of joy and meaning comes from work and 10% from outside of work; and then there are other seasons when the ratios are reversed (it could also be 80/20 or 70/30 or just about any other ratio other than 50/50). Ideally in the big picture and by the end of one's career, hopefully there has been an equal amount of joy and meaning from both. This is certainly a different conception of balance. However, this does not mean you should ever concede vacations and needed time off.

The difference between work-life integration and work-life *balance* may merely be semantics, but the argument is that work and life should each be considered necessary for contentment and joy in the other. Work is a necessary part of life and vice versa, and any stress may be the result of trying to separate 2 things (work and life) that cannot or should not be separated. In fact, Kanter[4] stated that to pursue work-life balance is to promote the "myth of separate spheres."

Whether you agree that work and life are mutually exclusive does not negate the issue of long work hours, nor does it mitigate the impact of the factors that contribute to burnout. Therefore, it is necessary to explore behaviors that can decrease burnout among health care professionals. Linzer et al[1] has identified 10 steps, organized into 4 areas (institutional measures, working conditions, career development, and self-care) aimed at decreasing burnout among medical professionals. These steps include:

Institutional Measures
1. Require clinician satisfaction and wellbeing in all quality indicators.
2. Incorporate mindfulness and teamwork into practice.
3. Decrease stress from electronic health records (ie, specifically the increased stress from increased computer time).

Work Conditions
4. Allocate resources to primary care clinics (reducing health care disparities).
5. Require clinician "floats" to cover predictable life events.
6. Give clinicians control of their work environment (eg, staff, schedules, patient loads).
7. Maintain manageable primary care practice sizes and enhanced staffing ratios.

Career Development
8. Preserve clinician "career fit" by protecting time for meaningful activities.
9. Promote part-time careers and job sharing within health care.

Self-Care
10. Make self-care a part of medical and health care professionalism.

Discussion Questions

1. Do you believe it is possible to go through an entire health care career without experiencing the consequences of burnout? Why?

2. What is the most important thing you believe you can do to decrease burnout and enhance the quality of your personal life outside of work?

3. What attitudes or beliefs do you think could be adopted that might contribute toward enhanced effectiveness at work and at home? How might considering the integration of work-life vs balance of work-life help?

4. What types of stress or tension do you feel the most when it comes to the tension between expectations of work and personal pursuits?

5. How would you describe the fundamental differences between the concepts of work-life integration vs work-life balance?

References

1. Linzer M, Levine R, Meltzer D, Poplau S, Warde C, West CP. 10 bold steps to prevent burnout in general internal medicine. *J Gen Intern Med.* 2014;29(1):18-20.

2. Kalliath T, Brough P. Work–life balance: a review of the meaning of the balance construct. *Journal of Management & Organization.* 2008;14(3):323-327.

3. Bailyn L, Fletcher JK. The equity imperative: reaching effectiveness through the dual agenda. Simmons Web site. http://www.simmons.edu/~/media/Simmons/About/CGO/Documents/INsights/Insights-18.ashx?la=en. Published July, 2003. Accessed July 31, 2017.

4. Kanter RM. *Work and Family in the United States: A Critical Review and Agenda for Research and Policy.* New York, NY: Russell Sage Foundation; 1977.

SECTION V

QUESTIONS ABOUT ORGANIZATIONAL CULTURE AND COMPLEXITY

QUESTION 22

My Professional Involvement Is Clinical—What More Do I Need to Know About Leadership?

One of the most frequent questions I receive from alumni relates to organizational dynamics. For example, I routinely ask alumni (my own and others), now that you have been working as a clinician, what is one thing that you wish you would have learned as a student? Rarely, perhaps never, do they respond with "more clinical skills." Almost always, the response is a nonclinical skill, such as developing and maintaining professional relationships, interpersonal communication, strategic planning, or something similar. I often follow-up by asking if they are sure they didn't want to learn another way to assess the knee or write an injury report. After their courtesy chuckle, the typical response goes something like this: "No, I've got that down, what I really wish I knew was to handle a difficult physician, market a new idea, ask for a promotion, or work with nontraditional stakeholders."

Interestingly, this response is extremely consistent with literature from nursing, medicine, and other clinical specialties.[1,2,3] In fact, Yule et al[3] identify the need for nonclinical skills of health care clinicians in 4 key areas:

1. Communication
2. Teamwork
3. Leadership
4. Decision making

Athletic training researchers have stated that, despite "excellent academic preparation" practicing athletic trainers (novices) have gaps in "professional communication, organization, and administration."[4] Likewise, literature in medicine states, on graduation, physicians are ready and able to diagnose and treat, but are not ready to practice.[5] Traditionally, health care education programs do an excellent job preparing clinicians, but a less than stellar job preparing professionals for the complex health care environment they are about to enter into. Developing the nonclinical skills needed to be successful in health care requires understanding complexity. For example, outside of health care, it has been reported that the success of an organization is limited to the degree one understands the complexity of the relationship between an organization and its environment.[6]

Kutz MR. *Leadership Questions for Health Care Professionals:*
Applying Theories & Principles to Practice (pp 79-94).
© 2018 SLACK Incorporated.

Navigating Organizational Complexity

The first step in developing needed nonclinical skills is to recognize the culture and climate that is created when the local environment and organization converge. Health care is an extremely complex environment to navigate.[7,8,9] This cannot be overstated. In fact, it is believed that health care is one of most complex environments in any society.[8]

New clinicians are typically overwhelmed by the level of complexity they face when entering the workforce. Perhaps this is because so much of clinical education and formal university courses are developed to minimize the complexity the student must navigate independent from instructors and preceptors, which in retrospect may not be helping the student understand organizational complexity. Complexity is not bad.[10] In fact, complexity adds richness and value to life, but it is often mistaken for confusion, so it is avoided or oversimplified.

What is organizational complexity? Organizational complexity comes from having multiple stakeholders with different, and sometimes competing values; and refers to something with many interactive parts, where the outcomes of those interactions vary widely and are unpredictable. Ironically, this is the opposite of the outcomes hoped for in evidence-based practice, which is to have small variance with predictable outcomes. Clinical decision-making rules and models may work with interventions studied on patients in controlled environments. These are considered complicated problems and as such, with the proper controls in place, variables, biases, and confounding factors can be identified and isolated. However, this process does not work with complexity. The foundational premise of complexity precludes isolation of variables. In fact, the 2 (complicated systems and complex systems) are governed by completely different "rules of engagement." It's as if patients are ruled by the laws of Newtonian physics, which govern complicated systems, where pieces and parts of the system can be isolated and replaced; while organizations are ruled by quantum physics, which governs complex systems, where once integrated, parts cannot be isolated. The 2 systems operate simultaneously, but are incompatible. I would suggest that the frustration associated with a lack of nonclinical skills is really the absence of understanding the tension between complex and complicated systems. The health care clinician has learned skills to help solve complicated problems (eg, budgeting, time management, clinical prediction rules), but not how to navigate complex organizations.

As if that is not enough, organizations are not only complex, but are also what many refer to as volatile, uncertain, complex, ambiguous (VUCA).[11] VUCA environments are incredibly difficult to navigate. Not because of inherent difficulty, but because of our existing mental maps. Most people's mental maps do not allow for the fact that some things cannot be simplified; there are always outliers that must be accounted for; that average is an artificial concept with value only in theoretical or abstract notions; that living organisms or ecosystems do not respond in predictable patterns, and yet are still patterned; and complex systems actually self-organize and external input usually creates a less than optimal outcome.

We can blame this, at least in part, on clinical education models that are designed to provide a specific experience as safely as possible. I'm not implying that should not be the case, but it does not represent reality, and consequently, new clinicians require a larger learning curve when entering the workplace. At some point, educational preparation must prepare future professionals for the volatility and uncertainty of the health care environment, and not relegate it to only on-the-job training.

This means faculty must update their often antiquated view of organizations and workplace culture, and that faculty must convey to students the organizational dynamics of health care. Specifically, organizations are not static, and every time a decision is made or an action is executed, the organization as an ecosystem responds. It is absolutely imperative to understand organizations as a living ecosystem. For example, in a natural ecosystem, removing a tiny organism that appears inconsequential eventually destroys that ecosystem; so too can "changing the type of gauze pad" totally disrupt (sometimes to the point of anarchy) a complex organization. If we treat organizations and our relationship within them as if they are a complicated or closed system, new clinicians will continue to be frustrated and require longer learning curves.

Types of Complexity

Birkinshaw and Heywood[10] state that not all complexity is equally manageable and identified 4 common types:

1. **Imposed complexity** includes laws, industry regulations, and interventions by federal and nongovernmental organizations. It is not typically manageable by companies.
2. **Inherent complexity** is intrinsic to the organization or industry, and can only be jettisoned by exiting or overhauling to the point of not recognizing a portion of the industry or organization.
3. **Designed complexity** results from choices about where the organization operates, what it sells/promotes, to whom, and how. Organizations can remove it, but this could mean simplifying valuable wrinkles in their operational model.
4. **Unnecessary complexity** arises from growing misalignment between the needs of the organization and the processes supporting it. It is easily managed once identified.

Discussion Questions

1. How can you begin to leverage the concept of complexity in your current practice (or clinical experiences)?
2. Put into your own words the difference between complex and complicated systems.
3. What strategies would you use to solve a complicated problem (one where contributing variables are easy to identify and isolate), and what would you do differently to solve a complex problem (one where contributing variables cannot be isolated)?
4. Review/recall a recent clinical experience. What clinical skills did you need/use and what nonclinical skills did you need/use?
5. What nonclinical skills do you observe experts using in their clinical environment?
6. What nonclinical skills do you believe are your strengths and what are weaknesses?

References

1. Daly WM. Critical thinking as an outcome of nursing education. What is it? Why is it important to nursing practice? *J Adv Nurs*. 1998;28(2):323-331.
2. Cherry MG, Fletcher I, O'Sullivan H, Dornan T. Emotional intelligence in medical education: a critical review. *Med Educ*. 2014;48(5):468-478.
3. Yule S, Flin R, Paterson-Brown S, Maran N. Non-technical skills for surgeons in the operating room: a review of the literature. *Surgery*. 2006;139(2):140-149.
4. Thrasher AB, Walker SE, Hankemeier DA, Pitney WA. Supervising athletic trainers' perceptions of professional socialization of graduate assistant athletic trainers in the collegiate setting. *J Athl Train*. 2015;50(3):321-333.
5. Parekh P, Ansari H. Residents more confident in clinical skills than nonclinical. *Ophthalmology Times*. 2007;32(7):64-67.

6.   Al-Zoubi MR. Leadership competencies and competitive advantage empirical study on Jordan telecommunications. *European Journal of Business and Management.* 2012;4(7):234-247.

7.   Sweeney K, Griffiths F. *Complexity and Healthcare: An Introduction.* London, United Kingdom: Radcliffe Medical Press; 2002.

8.   Begun JW, Thygeson M. Managing complex healthcare organizations. In: Fottler MD, Malvey D, Slovensky DJ, eds. *Handbook of Healthcare Management.* Cheltenham, United Kingdom: Edward Elgar Publishing; 2015.

9.   Sturmberg JP, Martin C. *Handbook of Systems and Complexity in Health.* New York, NY: Springer Science & Business Media; 2013.

10. Birkinshaw J, Heywood S. Putting organizational complexity in its place. *McKinsey Quarterly.* 2010;3(6):228.

11. Hernandez JS, Allen TC. Transformation of pathologists: responding in a volatile, uncertain, complex, and ambiguous environment. *Arch Pathol Lab Med.* 2013;137(5):603-605.

QUESTION 23

How Can I Figure Out What the Unwritten Rules Are, and How Can I Diagnose the Organizational Culture Around Here?

Organizational culture is a powerful concept that has a profound impact on employees. It is important to note that organizational culture is distinct from culture describing diversity or ethnicity. *Organizational culture* is a pattern of basic assumptions that are considered valid and are taught to new members as a way to perceive, think, and feel within the organization.[1] Every organization's culture has 3 levels of expression: artifacts, which are symbols of culture in the physical and social work environment; values, which are the stated beliefs of an organization; and thirdly, assumptions, which are unstated beliefs that guide member behaviors.

It is incumbent upon every health care professional to be able to diagnose or identify salient features of his or her organizational culture. Failing to identify an organization's culture often leads to frustration, anxiety, and ultimately lower retention. Schein[2] identified 3 levels of organizational culture: artifacts, values, and basic assumptions. Artifacts include things like ceremonies and rituals, rites of passage, stories, and symbols. These artifacts are often highly visible within the organization, but not very decipherable to outsiders. Example of artifacts within health care would include things like dress code rules, use of symbols (eg, white lab coats, stethoscope), stories that are consistently told about how a particular boss who is "human" or a particular employee who "saved the day," or stories about what happened to the last person who did "this." Other artifacts include rituals, such as retirement dinners, opening board meetings with prayer, and the annual company picnic. All of these are artifacts and other superficial indications of the organization's culture. These artifacts are highly visible, missing them is inexcusable, but they are not necessarily easy to decipher.

The second level of an organizations culture is its values. Values have a high level of awareness both internally and externally. Values can be tested within the environment and through social consensus. Values are often consciously articulated both in casual conversation and informal documents. However, it is important to note that there is often a difference between an organization's espoused values (what people say the values are) and its actual values (what the actual behaviors are). Many organizations publicly display their core values. It is important when diagnosing an organizations culture to recognize if their espoused values are consistent with the artifacts you have observed. For example, an organization may claim to have the core value of employee engagement, but fails to have any artifacts, such as retirement dinners, company picnics, or rewards for high-performing employees. Another example would be to have a stated value of patient satisfaction, but yet have a majority of decisions be driven by financial outcomes. Consistency between values can be valuable input when it comes to diagnosing an organization's culture.

Finally, the deepest level of organizational culture is its basic assumptions. These assumptions are deeply held beliefs that guide behavior and tell members of the organization how to perceive reality.[2] Basic assumptions are the unwritten rules that people within the culture take for granted. Basic assumptions are almost never included in a training program or orientation. They are deep undercover assumptions that entrenched members know to be true. Many times these assumptions are so deep that even those who are most engaged in them are unaware of them. According to Schein,[2] these assumptions are the most telling aspects of culture. Cawsey and colleagues[3] recommend, when trying to determine underlying assumptions of organizations, to ask questions about how the organization orients itself to time (ie, past, present, and future), and how those time orientations impact business. For example, what is the value of experience? How is experience valued and how is experience determined. In some organizations, it is possible for a novice to have relevant experience, and in others it is not. How are things like experience evaluated and defined? Additionally, Cawsey and colleagues[3] recommend asking about general assumptions relative to the nature of people. For example, is intelligence or personality fixed, or are they both something that can be developed over time? Undoubtedly, getting at basic underlying assumptions is the most difficult of the 3 levels to diagnose, but is certainly the most revealing.

Obviously, organizational culture is a very complex and dynamic concept. There are a considerable number of variables that contribute to organizational culture. Therefore, it is necessary to take the diagnostic process one step at a time. Before anyone can seriously engage in the task of diagnosing the organization's culture they must first, identify the artifacts; second, identify espoused vs actual values; and third, uncover any basic assumptions within their organization. Basic assumptions are the most difficult to uncover as they are embedded deep within the organization's culture. The obvious place to begin is with an organization's artifacts.

Discussion Questions

1. Identify some of the artifacts in your organization's culture that mean something to you but might be foreign to an outsider.

2. What are the espoused values that contribute to culture in your organization?

3. Is there a difference between your organization's espoused values and actual values? If so, what are they?

4. If you were asked, could you identify the unwritten rules and expectations that contribute to the culture within your organization?

5. Have you have ever taken the time to seriously consider your basic underlying assumptions about people and time (consider these "deeper" questions as a way to get started)?

    a. Have you ever thought, "there is no time for that", or "I could never do that (eg, finish my novel, receive my undergraduate degree, get out of debt) because there's not enough time"?

b. Have you ever considered your basic underlying assumption of how one gains experience and, more importantly, what experiences are important? Have you ever discounted someone, inadvertently of course, because they didn't have the "right kind" of experience?

c. Have you ever taken the time to consider your unconscious beliefs about work ethic? In other words, do you believe that people are inherently lazy and need to be motivated and inspired or, that if left to themselves, people work hard and do the right thing?

References

1. Nelson DL, Quick JC. *ORGB⁵: Organizational Behavior.* Boston, MA: Cengage; 2016
2. Schein EH. *Organizational Culture and Leadership.* 4th ed. Hoboken, NJ: John Wiley & Sons; 2010.
3. Cawsey TF, Deszca G, Ingols C. *Organizational Change: An Action-Oriented Toolkit.* London, United Kingdom: Sage Publications; 2016.

QUESTION 24

What Is a VUCA Organization, and Why Does It Matter to Me?

When answering questions about organizational culture it is critical to introduce and understand the concept of a VUCA environment. VUCA is an acronym, which stands for *volatility, uncertainty, complexity, and ambiguity*. Hernandez and Allen[1] report that physicians are in the VUCA world, and as a consequence, old norms of "Command-and-Control" processes are not effective. Disch[2] also reports that nurses must deal with a VUCA environment where the rules that used to be acceptable are no longer acceptable. Surgeons Mackey and Schweitzer[3] state that there is not a more accurate description for the current state of United States health care than the acronym VUCA. Pharmacy researchers ask if health care is slithering into an inescapable VUCA vortex, while clinicians remain blissfully unaware of its potential hazards.[4] Understanding a VUCA environment is important because it requires a new or different way of interaction (Table 24-1). As noted by both medical and nursing literature, traditional rules are not effective.[1,2]

Looking at each letter in the acronym, you begin to understand why it is an accurate description of contemporary health care. *Volatility* is a reference to the dynamic properties and the fast rate of change within an environment. When an environment is unstable and responds to outside forces it is said to be volatile. To work in a volatile environment is to know that a reaction *will* happen, but not knowing *when* it will happen. This often contributes to people feeling uneasy, which contributes to the need for self-preservation.

Uncertainty is the absence of predictability. This is particularly problematic because people love to try and predict things and they love to predict things based on their experiences. Ironically, people tend to think that they are much better at predicting than they actually are,[5] which compounds the effect of uncertainty. In uncertain environments, people are hesitant to commit to what they say they believe (values). Uncertainty can breed fear in people because it undermines their experience, and more importantly, their sense of structure and security are threatened by it. This perceived threat contributes to people needing to feel in control, which may lead to overstating the significance of their experiences.

Complexity is the weaving (some might say "crashing") together of multiple factors, some known and others unknown, from different environments. Once integrated, their convergence creates a new environment that can't be undone. Due to the mixing together of several factors there is a high perception of chaos. This perception of chaos typically causes people to anticipate

TABLE 24-1		
SOLUTIONS FOR VUCA		
	POTENTIAL HAZARDS	**POTENTIAL SOLUTIONS**
VOLATILITY	High need for self-preservation	Articulate a clear and actionable vision for the future, and help people realize how they can contribute toward that future.
UNCERTAINTY	Threatens the usefulness of people's experience. Threatens people's sense of structure and security	Identify and articulate the usefulness of people's ideas. Encourage the use of ideas from outside work-related experiences.
COMPLEXITY	High degree of presumption and reactionary behavior	Encourage people to explore non-traditional interactions or alternative explanations.
AMBIGUITY	Failure to accurately differentiate between alternatives	Evaluate and encourage agility and resiliency.

patterns prematurely, by assuming the past will repeat itself, or worse, not wait for any pattern at all. This causes people to respond one of 2 ways: 1) acting impulsively or being reactionary; or 2) making false assumptions about what is really happening.

Finally, *ambiguity* is the absence of distinctiveness. When something is ambiguous, it is hard to distinguish or differentiate from something else. Ambiguity in our workplaces results in mis-reading what has happened, or the failure to interpret the multiple meanings of a single event.

The reason a VUCA reality can be so destructive is our human tendency to blame people for these inconsistencies and not the environment that we helped to created.

Discussion Questions

1. How has the VUCA environment impacted your workspace?
2. Can you identify anything that your organization has done to address the problems of the VUCA environment?
3. Which element of the VUCA environment (volatility, uncertainty, complexity, or ambiguity) is most difficult for you to handle?
4. Which element of the VUCA environment (volatility, uncertainty, complexity, or ambiguity) is the easiest for you to handle?
5. Which element of the VUCA environment (volatility, uncertainty, complexity, or ambiguity) is most difficult for your organization to address?

References

1. Hernandez JS, Allen TC. Transformation of pathologists: responding in a volatile, uncertain, complex, and ambiguous environment. *Arch Pathol Lab Med.* 2013;137(5):603-605.
2. Disch J. Participatory health care: perspective from a nurse leader. *J Participat Med.* 2009;1(1):e4.
3. Mackey DC, Schweitzer MP. The future of surgical care in the US: state surgical quality collaboratives, optimized perioperative care, and the perioperative surgical home. *ASA Newsletter.* 2014;78(12):10-13.
4. Unnikrishnan MK. Eminence or evidence? The volatility, uncertainty, complexity, and ambiguity in healthcare. *J Pharmacol Pharmacother.* 2017;8(1):1.
5. Tetlock P. *Expert Political Judgment: How Good Is It? How Can We Know?* Princeton, NJ: Princeton University Press; 2005.

QUESTION 25

Health Care Is so Multifaceted— How Can I Explain the Nuance of Complexity to Others?

Health care is complex.[1] In fact, the inherent complexity of the health care system is becoming ever more apparent.[2] Instead of fighting complexity, it is recommended that health care leaders use it to frame their practice of leadership.[1,2] Leaders who understand the reality of complexity solve problems differently than mechanistic, Newtonian-based, or cause-and-effect (transactional) leaders. Since the health care environment is naturally complex, it is not a viable option to treat it as a machine, despite the temptation. It is imperative that health care clinicians understand the basics of complexity including what it is and what it is not. The reality is that leaders cannot solve *complex problems* with *complicated methods*.

Complex problems have numerous contributing sources each with varying degrees of influence; and complex problems can be solved by any number of effective solutions ranging from good, better, to best. When left alone, the best option seems to naturally emerge, but our need to intervene often changes the natural trajectory away from the best solution. A complex problem never has just one right answer needing to be distinguished from other wrong answers. Despite this reality, it is tempting to try and solve complex problems by using complicated techniques. Complicated techniques are those processes leaders employ that seek to find a single correct answer. Obviously, this is a major problem with complicated-based thinking. For example, if the default assumption is that there is only one right answer, a leader or team will instinctively stop looking for the best (or a better) answer when a solution is found that will work. Solving problems with complicated methods means using techniques that isolate or quarantine individual components that are usually seen as contributing to or causing the problem. Once isolated, an attempt is made at fixing or replacing the "broken piece," and then reinserting it back into the larger system. The danger with that lies in assuming that you have lessened collateral damage or eliminated disruption to other parts of the machine. I trust, that you can see how these 2 ideas, complexity and complication, are incompatible.

Incorporating complexity into the practice of leadership will require a different way of thinking. Within a complex environment, traditional leadership models are not adequate, and are even "hopelessly out of date."[2,3,4] It is becoming clear that the complexity facing the current health care system cannot be solved by traditional leadership models.[5] In order to address leadership in a complex world it is necessary to move away from traditional approaches, models, and theories, and move toward a whole-systems view. Interestingly, complexity can be managed quite well when the framework by which one practices leadership is altered to accommodate a complex (vs complicated) reality. It is critical to move away from mechanistic concepts of leadership, which are often illustrated by phrases such as, "we are firing on all cylinders," or "we are functioning like a well-oiled machine." These metaphors are problematic, in that they are completely inadequate to describe the complexity within organizations. The first shift that leaders must make is to resist the idea that organizations are like machines, and embrace the idea that they are more like an ecosystem. Ecology, and not engineering, is the better metaphor for health care organizations.

As we discussed in the last chapter, the world is becoming increasingly VUCA. In environments that are highly complex, individuals run the risk of reacting too quickly or inappropriately because of the tendency to find and apply the first good solution instead of the best solution. The other major risk, in a futile attempt to decrease collateral damage, is to isolate (or quarantine) relevant factors during the decision-making process. However, like any ecosystem, when something is taken out, the entire environment suffers in ways that cannot be predicted. The inherent assumption is that by isolation, the risk of contamination or collateral damage can be reduced. So, we endeavor to keep things "simple." In this case simple usually means small, bite-sized, manageable units that can be easily diagnosed and replaced if necessary.

The opposite of complexity is not simplicity. Keeping things simple, does not mean they are not complex! In its basic sense, complexity means difficult to isolate or comprised of many parts. The true opposite of complex is separate (or discernible).

To review, complexity is the weaving together of multiple known and unknown factors. Once weaved together, a new reality emerges that can't be unwoven. The best way to understand complexity is to compare it to the concept of complicated. Something that is complicated is mechanical, like a car engine. A mechanistic, or complicated, view of the world implies that different parts fit together, and when those parts are not working they can be identified and then replaced or fixed. However, this is not true in a complex system. Something that is complex is woven together into a new, larger whole. If one of the original parts is not working well the consequence appears throughout the whole system (or somewhere else in the system) and is difficult to identify or isolate.

For example, a car engine is complicated, but a cake is complex. The car engine has many pieces that fit together. Likewise, a cake has many ingredients that are mixed together. In a car engine, parts retain their individuality, but in a cake ingredients do not. Once the cake ingredients have been mixed together, it becomes something new—batter. Once the batter is mixed, the eggs (or any other ingredient) cannot be isolated, removed, or replaced—this makes it complex. Not so with a car engine. Since it is a complicated machine, once assembled, broken pieces can still be identified and isolated apart form the whole. It works, but only with complicated systems. Trying to solve complex problems with complicated-based processes is like trying to remove the eggs from a baked cake. Understanding that health care is complex requires leaders and managers to interact with it differently.

Discussion Questions

1. Does your organization solve problems with complexity-based thinking or complicated-based thinking? Give an example.
2. How does/should thinking of health care as a complex system change the way health care is practiced?
3. Clinically, are there any correlations or relationships to complex systems and evidence-based practice or disablement models?
4. How might complexity-based thinking play a role in problem solving for each of the following situations:
    a. Improving a patient's treatment outcomes with fewer reimbursed contacts
    b. Handing a conflict between coworkers
    c. Improving patient satisfaction scores without affecting any costs

References

1. Lipsitz LA. Understanding health care as a complex system: the foundation for unintended consequences. *JAMA* 2012;308(3):243-244.
2. Weberg D. Complexity leadership: a healthcare imperative. *Nurs Forum.* 2012;47(4):268-277.
3. Kutz M. Embracing Complexity. In: Kutz M. *Contextual Intelligence: How Thinking in 3D Can Help Resolve Complexity, Uncertainty and Ambiguity.* Berlin, Germany: Springer International Publishing; 2017:55-70.
4. Uhl-Bien M, Marion R, McKelvey B. Complexity leadership theory: shifting leadership from the industrial age to the knowledge era. *Leadersh Q.* 2007;18(4):298-318.
5. Uhl-Bien M, Marion R. *Complexity Leadership: Part 1: Conceptual Foundations (Vol. 5).* Charlotte, NC: Information Age Publishing; 2008.

QUESTION 26

Does Leadership Work the Same Everywhere, and Can I Transfer My Leadership Skills Somewhere Else?

A direct answer to this question is *yes* and *no*. However, the question is more nuanced than it appears. Yes, leadership can work regardless of the environment if there is an agreed-upon definition. No, leadership does not always translate into other environments if it is a product of professional socialization.

To clarify, this question is asking if the leadership skills learned for work can be used effectively outside of work and if the leadership behaviors learned outside of the workplace can be used effectively at work. Many clinicians and health care administrators ask this question because of the conflicting literature and dialogue that is available on leadership. For example, there is ample literature to support the idea that everyone is a leader and everyone practices leadership.[1,2] Still, there is other literature that identifies specific steps for certain people on how to become a leader in a particular organization or industry. These send conflicting messages. On the one hand, leadership is for anybody anywhere regardless of their role or function within an organization. On the other hand, leadership is reserved for those who practice certain behaviors or abilities often, which can only be learned through professional socialization. There are several possible combinations one can take away from these 2 conflicting messages.

Some, combine these 2 messages and conclude that they can be a leader outside of work, but not at work; or they can be a leader at work, but not outside of work. Still others come away believing they can be a leader both at work and outside of work; and then, there are always those who are convinced they cannot be the leader anywhere. The underlying issue to which one of these messages is true is based on the presupposed definition of leadership. For the purposes of this book, we defined leadership in previous chapters, but that does not mean everyone is referencing the same operational definition when discussing leadership.

The answer of course is context-specific. To address this question adequately we must determine if leadership development is independent of, or in, collaboration with professional socialization. The response is important. If leadership is independent of professional socialization then, as we have said, leadership can be practiced by anyone and learned anywhere. If, on the other hand, leadership is part of professional socialization, then leadership must be taught within the formal constraint of professional development. Within organizations, especially health care organizations, the term leadership is used so haphazardly that there is often confusion about what it means. One should always ask which portrayal of leadership is being used; is it the type expected of a professional as part of a unique body of knowledge or the more general sense of leadership?

It is a mistake to assume that leadership means the same thing to everybody all the time, or that even the same person uses it the same way all the time. Often times the same person, same organization, or same profession uses the term leadership interchangeably (one way implies a unique professional behavior—and sometimes even technical competencies—and the other way implies common leadership behaviors), and rarely do they tell you in advance which aspect they are referencing.

Professional Socialization and Leadership

Professional socialization, sometimes called professionalism, is the process of acquiring values, attitudes, and skills thought to be important by a professional society or group and is part of a professional identity.[3] Within athletic training, socialization is said to be the process by which an individual learns the roles and responsibilities of his or her profession and emerges as a member of the professional culture.[4] One of the aspects of leadership that has been reported to be important within athletic training is the practice of scholarship.[5] It is important for athletic trainers, who want to be considered leaders within their profession, to practice scholarship; thus, scholarship is an expected outcome of an athletic trainer's professional education. It is unlikely to find "practicing scholarship" as an expected leadership behavior within a leadership training program for a car salesman or government employee. In this regard, there are leadership attributes that are unique to a particular environment, and therefore, the answer to our original question is no. However, as you can imagine, this is not the end of the discussion. There are leadership behaviors that are common and can be practiced regardless of the environment. For example, empathy or communication (there are many others and these are only examples).

These examples (ie, empathy and communication) are also expected of health care and allied health care professionals and are often an expected outcome of educational preparation, but they also transcend professional preparation and are an expectation of leaders everywhere, including car salesmen and government officials. Empathy can be learned, like many other leadership behaviors, outside of a formal professional's socialization process. This is often what leads to the confusion. When discussing leadership, what specifically do you mean by it; and once identified, where do you learn it? Do you mean the expected behaviors as a process of professional socialization, or do you mean some other more common or general behaviors that can be learned outside of the formal socialization process? Being on the proverbial same page when discussing leadership with anybody is crucial for avoiding misunderstandings.

Leadership when discussed within the purview of professional socialization often gets convoluted with similar constructs like management, administration, and professional behaviors. Consequently, the professional is often confused about what leadership actually is and how it can be developed. For example, attending a continuing education course on strategic planning, policymaking, diversity, or budgeting is not necessarily leadership development as much as it is professional socialization. By considering professional development (or socialization) to be equivalent to leadership development we shortchange leadership, and often neglect to see how leadership behaviors can have a wider impact. On the other hand, this is typically not the case when engaged in purely leadership development programs that teach things like empathy, initiative, and communication.

Discussion Questions

1. What are the different understandings of leadership that you have encountered?
2. How is leadership that you are being taught in school different from how it is practiced in the marketplace?
3. What is the problem with using technical competencies as inclusion criteria for leadership behaviors?
4. How does mixing professional behaviors, management expectations, and leadership behaviors complicate the leadership development processes? Should they stand alone?
5. How is the leadership development process different from professional socialization, and how might they be similar?

References

1. Arya D. So, you must be a leader-everyone is! *Asia Pacific Journal of Health Management.* 2014;9(2):8.
2. Shelton K. *A New Paradigm of Leadership: Visions of Excellence for 21st Century Organizations.* Provo, UT: Executive Excellence Publishing; 1997.
3. Zarshenas L, Sharif F, Molazem Z, Khayyer M, Zare N, Ebadi A. Professional socialization in nursing: a qualitative content analysis. *Iran J Nurs Midwifery Res.* 2014;19(4):432-438.
4. Klossner J. The role of legitimation in the professional socialization of second-year undergraduate athletic training students. *J Athl Train.* 2008;43(4):379-385.
5. Kutz MR. Leadership in athletic training: implications for practice and education in allied health care. *J Allied Health.* 2010;39(4):265-279.

SECTION VI

QUESTIONS ABOUT LEADERSHIP ETHICS AND POWER

QUESTION 27

I Know Ethics Is Important, but Do I Need to Worry About Ethical Leadership? Shouldn't That Be Natural?

Yes, ethics is important. Yes, ethics is something you should be intentional about. No, being ethical is not natural. The need to improve health care is urgent. However, Faden and colleagues[1] says the current ethics paradigm may be an obstacle to improving it. The current paradigm, at least in part, considers ethics deeply personal and therefore, people are not comfortable discussing it is a matter of public discourse. Dye[2] claims that many people are uncomfortable discussing ethics because it "reveals private opinions." Another issue is the assumption that people are inherently ethical and as a consequence of this assumption, ethical errors are often considered accidental mistakes. Subsequently, it is difficult (or not necessary) to create policy or be proactive. This could be remedied if people were willing to admit that ethical behavior is not natural to the human condition. In support of that, Hofmann[3] suggests that ethical fallout occurs as a natural byproduct of people's innate tendency to need to avoid conflict. In other words, people do not confront unethical behavior in order to ensure self-preservation.

Within the context of sports medicine, several ethical issues have been reported including confidentiality, return-to-play decisions, conflicts of interest, advertising, doping, and use of local anesthetic.[4] Some common issues resulting in ethical dilemmas for nurses include providing less than optimal care due to management decisions, seeing patient care suffer due to lack of provider continuity, and working with others who are less than competent.[5] Most professional organizations, especially those within health care, have codes of ethics that practicing clinicians are obligated to adhere to. Unfortunately, these codes of ethics are rather vague, principle driven, and do not delineate specific behaviors to be avoided. As such, there is confusion and personal interpretation in what constitutes ethical and unethical behavior. In addition to adhering to organizational codes of ethics, Dye[2] suggests adding the following measures to help ensure ethical behavior within the health care industry. These behaviors include:

Kutz MR. *Leadership Questions for Health Care Professionals:*
Applying Theories & Principles to Practice (pp 97-103).
© 2018 SLACK Incorporated.

- **Write a personal code of ethics**: A personal code of ethics establishes the values that are important to you and helps to prioritize difficult decisions.
- **Commit to never exaggerate:** This includes refusing to overestimate, engage in hyperbole, or embellish the facts; it means committing to not overstate or understate an issue and refusing to misquote to support your point.
- **Always do what you say you will do:** Follow through on what you say you will do.
- **Never abuse power:** Understand the sources of power and use them appropriately.
- **Always admit mistakes:** Admitting mistakes is not weakness, power is earned incrementally and is easier to attain if you are willing to admit mistakes.
- **Be willing to march to the beat of your own drum:** Understand and practice your own set of personal values and refuse to make decisions based on popular opinion.
- **Be trustworthy:** Honor commitments and promises and be sure that your behavior aligns with espoused values.
- **Manage expense accounts judiciously:** Never use access to funds or resources for personal reasons. In every case, supply receipts and reports for expenses.

Beyond the personal ethical safeguards suggested by Dye[2], Faden and colleagues[1] provide an overarching framework for ethical behavior in a health care system that is committed to continual improvement. Slightly different from Dye's recommendations are the 7 obligations outlined by Faden and colleagues,[1] which are intended to be initiated, administered, and assessed by organizations (and not necessarily individuals):

1. Respecting the rights and dignity of patients
2. Respecting the clinical judgment of peers
3. Providing optimal (most benefits with fewest risks) care to each patient
4. Avoiding imposing nonclinical risks and burdens on patients
5. Reducing health inequalities among populations
6. Conducting responsible activities that foster learning from clinical care and clinical information
7. Contributing to the common purpose of improving the quality and value of clinical care and health care systems

Discussion Questions

1. After an honest appraisal of your attitudes and values, what issues are you willing to compromise, and on which issues will you never compromise?
2. Are you inherently an ethical person, or do you (or have you ever) put your interests before others?
3. Can you put your interests before others and still be ethical?
4. Do you always act in the best interest of your patients, regardless of what that means for you or your employer?
5. When have you violated any of Dye's ethical safeguards?
6. What are some of the most common ethical dilemmas you wrestle with?

7. What are some of the most common or typical ethical dilemmas you notice that your peers and colleagues wrestle with?
8. How might leadership be able to assist with handling ethical dilemmas?

References

1. Faden RR, Kass NE, Goodman SN, Pronovost P, Tunis S, Beauchamp TL. An ethics framework for a learning health care system: a departure from traditional research ethics and clinical ethics. *Hastings Center Report.* 2013;43(s1):S16-S27.
2. Dye CF. *Leadership in Healthcare: Essential Values and Skills.* Chicago, IL: Health Administration Press; 2017.
3. Hofmann PB. Fear of conflict: management and ethical costs: wanting to avoid conflict is natural but should not inhibit appropriate behavior. *Healthcare Executive.* 2012;27(1):58.
4. Riendeau C, Parent-Houle V, Lebel-Gabriel ME, et al. An investigation of how university sports team athletic therapists and physical therapists experience ethical issues. *J Orthop Sports Phys Ther.* 2015;45(3):198-206.
5. Woods M, Rodgers V, Towers A, La Grow S. Researching moral distress among New Zealand nurses: a national survey. *Nurs Ethics.* 2015;22(1):117-130.

QUESTION 28

How Can I Get More Power at Work Without Manipulating People? Is That Even Possible?

Power is an incredibly simple concept that can have a profound impact on a person or organization. Power has been defined as the ability to affect others' beliefs, attitudes, and behaviors.[1,2] Being able to affect other people's beliefs, attitudes, and behaviors is an extremely valuable commodity and is used by everybody to varying degrees. Avoiding or neglecting the use of power can be detrimental.[3] Failing to understand how power is acquired within the workplace can be a disadvantage, likewise understanding how power is acquired and using it can be a tremendous advantage. Interestingly, the concept of power is often used interchangeably with influence. In fact, some people prefer the term *influence* over *power* because power can, at times, have a negative connotation. What are the different types of power, and how can you use them effectively?

In a seminal work by French and Raven[4] they identified 5 sources of power, to which Raven[1] later added a sixth. The 6 types of power include:

1. **Legitimate power**: consists of compliance to requests, and is based on the assumption that an individual has the formal right to make demands and to expect compliance.

2. **Reward power**: consists of compliance as a result of expected reward or compensation. This type of power is held by individuals who have control over the disbursement of resources.

3. **Expert power**: consists of compliance as a result of specialized knowledge in a particular domain. This type of power is dependent upon an individual's high level of skill and knowledge.

4. **Referent power**: consists of compliance because a person is liked, admired, or respected. This type of power is held by individuals that others consider to be role models, mentors, or admirable.

5. **Coercive power**: consists of compliance out of fear of retribution. This type of power is the opposite of reward power, and is held by people who have the authority to withhold resources or punishments.

6. **Informational power**: consists of compliance because of one's skill in utilizing information to provide logical or persuasive arguments. This type of power is held by individuals who have access to or control over information that people need.

Why Do We Not Have Power?

Jeffrey Pfeffer,[3] professor at Stanford University Graduate School of Business (Stanford, California) and perhaps the world's leading expert on power, identified 3 barriers to the use of power. Barrier number one is the belief that the world is "fair and just," and consequently, people often are not as strategic or vigilant as needed. Pfeffer[3] cites that the reason for this is the "Just World Hypothesis,"[5,6] which is the need to believe that the environment is a just and orderly place where people usually get what they deserve. Pfeffer[3] posits that this belief makes people less powerful by limiting their willingness to learn from all situations and all people; and by anesthetizing them to the need to proactively build power. He suggests that people who believe the world is fair typically fail to see the land mines in their path.

The second barrier to power that Pfeffer identifies is the "leadership literature." Pfeffer[3] argues that much of the leadership literature is based on how people (ie, scholars and practitioners) believe leaders should behave, and is not based on how they actually do behave. Most of the time, people who have achieved high levels of leadership success have done so by demonstrating power, however, the use of power is rarely offered as an explanation. Pfeffer[3] believes that in addition to leadership competencies (he does not discount them), power often plays a larger role than it is initially given credit for. Therefore, the wholesale application of leadership concepts, without considering all the possible implications contributes to underestimating the significance power has in practicing leadership.

Finally, the third barrier that Pfeffer[3] identifies to the practice of power is "delicate self-esteem." In most cases, people are their own worst enemies.[3] By intentionally neglecting to pursue or demonstrate power, one can protect their ego when they do not get it by telling themselves that they would have gotten it had they tried. People lie to themselves about their desire or need for power and even put obstacles in their own path; therefore, when they do not obtain it, they do not have to consider it a personal failure.

Ways to Attain Power

Citing decades of research, Pfeffer[3] identified several ways to exercise power effectively. Table 28-1 identifies some of the more basic aspects of how to leverage power effectively.

TABLE 28-1
ENHANCING THE USE OF POWER

TECHNIQUE FOR EXERCISING POWER	DESCRIPTION
Distribute resources/Help people out	Helping people evokes reciprocity. When you do favors for other people, they invariably feel a sense of gratitude and often feel obligated to repay the favor.
Advance on multiple fronts	If you find an obstacle in the path toward your goal, find another route. Be sure to establish allies in several departments or areas.
Make the first move	Don't wait to see what happens or how something plays out. If you suspect change, be proactive in addressing it.
Co-opt antagonists	Make opponents and antagonists part of your team and offer them an opportunity to contribute.
Remove rivals	Gracefully, tactfully, and nicely help rivals find new or alternate employment.
Don't draw unnecessary fire	Do not create unnecessary opposition by inviting critique from peripheral or marginal stakeholders.
Use the personal touch	Always be polite and go out of your way to learn small and important details about the people around you.
Make important relationships work	Feelings change frequently between colleagues. Put aside resentment, jealousy, and any other negative attitude that might hinder you from getting your job accomplished.
Persist	Always practice diligence and dedication; consistency of effort and longevity help accumulate power.
Make the vision compelling	Place your personal objectives in the broader context that compels others around you to give you their support.

Discussion Questions

1. On a scale of 1 to 10, how effectively do you use each of the 6 types of power?
2. What type of power do you demonstrate most often?
3. What type of power do you most need to develop?
4. How has your use of power helped (or hurt) in achieving your goals?
5. Explain a situation when you should have used power to accomplish your goals, but didn't.
6. What types of power do people generally use on you?
7. Which barrier to power are you most susceptible to?
8. Of the different techniques for exercising power, which do you find the most interesting, and which do you find the most harmful?

References

1. Raven BH. Six bases of power. In: Goethals GR, MacGregor Burns J, Sorenson GJ, eds. *Encyclopedia of Leadership*. Thousand Oaks, CA: Sage Publications; 2004.
2. Bélanger JJ, Pierro A, Kruglanski AW. Social power tactics and subordinates' compliance at work: the role of need for cognitive closure. *Eur Rev Appl Psychol*. 2015;65(4):163-169.
3. Pfeffer J. Power play. Harvard Business Review Web site. 2010:84-92. https://hbr.org/2010/07/power-play. Published July, 2010. Accessed August 1, 2017.
4. French JRP, Raven BH. The bases of social power. In: Cartwright D, ed. *Studies in Social Powe*r. Ann Arbor, MI: Institute for Social Research; 1959.
5. Lerner MJ, Simmons CH. Observer's reaction to the "innocent victim": compassion or rejection? *J Pers Soc Psychol*. 1966:4(2):203.
6. Lerner MJ, Miller DT. Just world research and the attribution process: looking back and ahead. *Psychol Bull*. 1978;85(5):1030.

SECTION VII

QUESTIONS ABOUT DIVERSITY AND MULTICULTURAL LEADERSHIP

QUESTION 29

Really? Medical Tourism? Is That a Real Thing That Came From Globalized Health Care?

One of the more recent and major outcomes of globalization in health care is the phenomenon known as medical tourism.[1,2] Medical tourism is a rapidly emerging expression of a global commercialization of health care. It is simply described as traveling to other countries, usually lesser developed countries, for medical and health care treatment. The drivers behind medical tourism include: lower cost of health care in developing countries, especially for patients with no insurance or high premiums; avoidance of long wait times, especially for countries with the National Health Service (NHS) (eg, Britain and Canada); to acquire services not available in one's own country; privacy and confidentiality; and finally, and the least significant driver, desire to combine elective medical care with tourism.[3] Typically, the medical facilities in these developing countries offer luxurious accommodations and far superior customer service, which is a draw for privately insured or wealthy patients.

Traditionally, medical care has been supported and operated within the public's best interest within national borders. However, medical care has recently expanded beyond national borders, which is indicative of the emerging globalization within health care and specifically highlights the impact of privatized health care insurance.[2] Medical tourism shows no signs of slowing down. In fact, as health care becomes more and more complex within developed countries, there is a larger exodus of wealthy or privately insured individuals seeking health care in less developed countries. It is estimated that approximately 10.5 to 23.2 million people, most presumably from the United States, will seek medical care in developing countries by 2017.[1]

Lunt et al[4] point out that traveling abroad for health care is not new. People in developing nations have traveled to more developed countries for medical care and health benefits for centuries. However, what is new is citizens from wealthy, developed, or industrialized nations traveling to underdeveloped or developing nations for their health care. It is currently estimated that medical tourism generates over $60 billion in revenue annually and only show signs of increasing.[5] Just

Kutz MR. *Leadership Questions for Health Care Professionals:*
Applying Theories & Principles to Practice (pp 107-116).

about half of that revenue is said to be generated by India, and other countries for medical tourism include Thailand, Tunisia, China, Mexico, Singapore, and Malaysia.[5] Some of the most common procedures sought out in these countries include cosmetic surgery, dentistry, orthopedic and spine surgery, reproductive surgery, bariatric surgery, and cardiac surgery.[5]

The physicians and medical professionals who offer these services are very often highly trained, have the appropriate board certifications or equivalent, and often practiced in developed countries before relocating to lesser developed nations. Presumably, one of the drivers for physicians to relocate is more autonomy in medical decision, and ironically, higher quality of care or at least care that is not micromanaged by NHS, managed care organizations, or insurance companies.

Discussion Questions

1. What might you consider to be some of the key leadership implications of medical tourism?
2. What would facilitate you intentionally going to another country for medical care?
3. Would it benefit any of your patients to go overseas to seek medical/health care treatment?
4. How does your profession (or closely-related professions) practice overseas?
5. What are the professions that are related to what you do in health care called (and how are they trained) in other countries?
6. What would you need to do/learn to practice in another country?
7. What would a credentialed professional from another country need to do to be eligible to practice your profession in the United States?

References

1. Hopkins L, Labonté R, Runnels V, Packer C. Medical tourism today: what is the state of existing knowledge? *J Public Health Policy.* 2010;31(2):185-198.
2. Uchida Y. Medical tourism or 'medical examination and treatment abroad': an economic study of the phenomenon. In: Cooper M, Vafadari K, Hieda M, eds. *Current Issues and Emerging Trends in Medical Tourism.* Hershey, PA: IGI Global; 2015:18-30.
3. Horowitz MD, Rosensweig J. Medical tourism-health care in the global economy. *Physician Exec.* 2007;33(6):24-30.
4. Lunt N, Smith R, Exworthy M, Green ST, Horsfall D, Mannion R. Medical tourism: treatments, markets and health system implications: a scoping review. Organisation for Economic Co-operation and Development Web site. https://www.oecd.org/els/health-systems/48723982.pdf. Published 2011. Accessed August 1, 2017.
5. Horowitz MD, Rosensweig JA, Jones CA. Medical tourism: globalization of the healthcare marketplace. *MedGenMed.* 2007;9(4):33-40.

QUESTION 30

I Know It's Important, but Why Does Diversity and Cultural Competence Seem so Divisive?

Increasing the cultural and ethnic diversity of practicing clinicians is a major campaign within health care. Currently, there is a clear and present disparity of the quality of health care being offered to minority and ethnically diverse individuals.[1] It has been suggested that increasing diversity among health professionals can significantly help to improve access to care, increase patient satisfaction, and improve patient outcomes.[2] Therefore, hospitals, clinics, and health care systems are working diligently to increase the cultural diversity among health care professionals. However, the focus on diversity and cultural issues will challenge organizations in unpredictable ways,[3] which adds to the leadership uncertainty and volatility of the workplace.

While efforts towards greater cultural diversity among health care clinicians are being made, there is still a large disparity in the outcomes for minorities and ethnically diverse patients. There seems to be a larger issue facing health care than just recruiting more culturally diverse clinicians. Health care literature reports that multicultural leadership is one of the most frequently practiced leadership behaviors.[4] Yet, "embraces diverse ideas" is significantly lower in practice frequency comparatively. Kutz and colleagues[4] speculate that this gap is based in the reality that health care systems are recruiting and hiring clinicians from different cultures and ethnicities (hence the high degree of multicultural leadership), but are still making hiring selections based on candidates having similar experiences and backgrounds. The health care industry seems to be recruiting clinicians from different cultures, but when hiring them, the selection criteria is based on how similar their ideas, education, experience, and background are to their own. In essence, they end up with a "culturally diverse" team who all have similar backgrounds and experience, thus, nullifying any potential benefit of diversity. Perhaps we are misunderstanding the concept of diversity entirely, and in addition to adding cultural diversity to our health care teams, we should intentionally recruit health care professionals with different experiences and education as a priority, regardless of culture or ethnicity.

Refusing to hire people with diverse ideas can be problematic. Therefore, it is natural to ask, is there a reason we don't hire people with "idea diversity"? Given that health care is so highly regulated, the quality and rigor of a clinician's education and training must be taken into consideration. It is possible we are stuck between the proverbial "rock and a hard place," in that we call for diversity in practice, but do not allow for it during credentialing. For example, entry-level credentials, certifications, or licensure, are typically based on predetermined standards that require health care professionals within a specific domain to obtain nearly identical experiences. It is almost as if formal health care education educates the idea of diversity out of a person. If a student does not strictly adhere to predefined and predetermined experiences, they are not even eligible sit for licensure and certification exams. Cultural diversity is then left for extracurricular development or is relegated to advanced practice (that is reserved for professionals who have already achieved entry-level recognition). Novel and innovative educational programs within health care may require study abroad or an international experience in their curriculum, but that is still rare. It is arguable that the growing emphasis on interprofessional education and practice is an intermediate step or perhaps even a surrogate for "true" cultural competency and diversity.

Much of health care education is based on having similar competencies and uniform clinical education. Many health care professionals who have diverse experiences, different education, or different backgrounds may not meet the educational standards and rigor required to practice health care within the United States. Furthermore, many of the skills that a truly diverse health care team might bring to the proverbial "table" are likely not to be reimbursed by insurance companies and therefore may not be considered as valuable or even necessary services.

The issue of diversity and culturally competent care goes well beyond simply hiring people with different skin colors or countries of origin. The real issue within health care is to enable a creative process whereby clinicians with diverse experience, theories, and philosophies of care, are allowed to work together on patient centered care. It is misleading and shortsighted to assume that the only diversity is cultural—but obviously it is a major component to diversity and remains the best place to start. It may become necessary to consider alternative recruitment and hiring strategies if health care is to truly diversify.

Despite the disconnect in the different conceptions of diversity, it is still important for health care professionals to begin to practice recommended behaviors that have been shown to increase culturally competent care. Douglas and colleagues[5] outlined a detailed list of behaviors to help health care professionals practice culturally competent health care. Those behaviors include:

- **Learn new things about different cultures:** Be intentional about traveling abroad and studying with clinicians who are educated and trained in other countries. Learn about the cultural heritage and religions of other countries.

- **Participate in education and training for administering culturally competent care:** Learn about the expectations, including worldviews, other cultures bring to health care.

- **Critical reflection:** Intentionally reflect on your own beliefs and attitudes about quality health care, and how they might be different from what a person from another country would expect.

- **Cross-cultural communication:** Intentionally seek out opportunities to dialogue with patients and colleagues who were educated and trained in other countries.

- **Engage in culturally competent practices:** Once you identify a culturally diverse behavior try it out.

- **Advocate for cultural competence in health care systems:** Be a champion for cultural competency in the workplace, don't assume someone else will do it.

- **Advocate for culturally diverse patients:** Be diligent about making sure that patients who do come from other countries are having their expectations met, which may mean extended dialogue as often their expectations are "unspoken."

- **Intentionally engage a multicultural workforce:** Seek out colleagues to practice alongside of who are from different cultures.

- **Practice cross cultural leadership:** When solving problems and making decisions be sure to work alongside colleagues from other countries.
- **Practice evidence-based practice:** Remember that evidence-based practice includes the clinicians experience and patient's values and expectations, it does not only consist of high-quality clinical research.

I would also add to not be afraid to mess up. I am not talking about being negligent, but much like people from a foreign country appreciate it when you try to speak their language, people are generally accepting and understanding of efforts made to help them feel more at home, even if you mess it up. Perhaps even a more simplified way to begin practicing culturally competent health care within a diverse team is to apply what Heaslip[6] refers to as the ABCs of culturally competent health care:

- **A=Attitude:** Being open to seeing, valuing, and appreciating another person's view of the world, which is likely to be different from your own.
- **B=Behavior:** Acting in a way that validates and respects different cultural beliefs. Adjusting ones behavior to accommodate the others perspective.
- **C=Communication:** Always ask colleagues, "Is there anything that you think I need to know about you or your beliefs in order to work with you?"

Discussion Questions

1. What do you do to intentionally practice culturally competent care in your workplace?
2. What policies or recommendations does your organization have in place to ensure that culturally competent health care is occurring?
3. Does a patient need to have a health care provider who is of the same race or ethnicity as them to receive the best possible care?
4. Do you think there's more value in having a health care team who is diverse culturally but tends to think the same way, or a team who is similar ethnically but has a wide range of different experiences and diverse backgrounds?
5. Consider comment on the following scenario: Team 1 consists of 2 physicians, one physician is from India and the other South Africa, and both attended Ivy League schools in the United States and completed their residencies at the same hospital within the same discipline. Team 2 is also comprised of 2 physicians, both from the United States (both from the same undergraduate institution); one attended medical school in Great Britain while the second attended medical school in South Africa, one completed post-doctoral residency training with the World Health Organization touring northern Africa, while the second completed training at a large metropolitan hospital in the United States. Which team is more diverse?
6. I've been fortunate to be able to practice clinically in several countries. I spent the most time, 6 months, in Rwanda. The clinicians there were well-trained and extremely competent; however, if they were to come to the United States, they would have great difficulty being able to practice due to licensure and degree requirements. How does this present an obstacle to culturally competent health care? Please discuss possible solutions to issues similar to this.

References

1. Betancourt JR, Green AR, Carrillo JE, Ananeh-Firempong O. Defining cultural competence: a practical framework for addressing racial/ethnic disparities in health and health care. *Public Health Rep.* 2003;118(4):293-302.
2. Rigsby J. *Promoting Cultural Diversity in Allied Healthcare Programs: A Case Study* [doctoral dissertation]. Tempe, AZ: University of Phoenix; 2016.
3. Cawsey TF, Deszca G, Ingols C. *Organizational Change: An Action-Oriented Toolkit.* Thousand Oaks, CA: Sage Publications; 2016.
4. Kutz MR, Ball DA, Carroll GK. Contextual intelligence behaviors of female hospital managers in the United States. *International Journal of Healthcare Management.* 2017:1-9. doi: 10.1080/20479700.2017.1309819
5. Douglas MK, Rosenkoetter M, Pacquiao DF, et al. Guidelines for implementing culturally competent nursing care. *J Transcult Nurs.* 2014;25(2):109-121.
6. Heaslip V. Caring for people from diverse cultures. *Br J Community Nurs.* 2015;20(9):421-421.

QUESTION 31

Seriously, I Have Enough to Learn and Manage, and Now I Need to Be Concerned About Different Cultures' Worldviews? Okay, What Are They?

It is certainly easier than any other time in history to learn things about different cultures, but few things compare to the impact of an interactive international experience. I have read books, articles, and watched documentaries on countries where I was planning to travel, but have consistently found them woefully inadequate in conveying the reality of that country. The fact is so much of what we see and read about other countries in preparation for going to that country is through the lens of our own culture and worldview. More often than not, this blinds us to reality (this is not only true of different cultures, but our worldview filters what we believe about our neighbors also). It is nearly impossible to get a fair and accurate view of another person's beliefs and practices without actually being there to witness them firsthand. Obviously, everyone cannot travel abroad for clinical education experiences. Therefore, it is incumbent upon us as culturally competent health care professionals to learn as much as we can about other countries, but not just facts—we must be willing to learn the much more important and impactful reality concerning different worldviews. Learning about different worldviews may be the next best thing to actually going there, and it is certainly more valuable than learning facts and data points about different cultural customs. Without understanding the worldview that informs and gives meaning to the custom, knowing about the custom is worthless.

Technically defined, *cultural competence* is the capacity of an individual to incorporate ethnic and cultural considerations of diverse coworkers and patients into his or her work and care. *Globalization* is the exchange and integration of cultural ideals, social ideals, values, politics, and technologies between diverse people or groups as a result of increased access.[1] Globalization's concept of integration transcends superficial acts of inclusion, such as wishing someone "happy holidays" in lieu of "Merry Christmas," and fundamentally requires integrating behaviors that the other person considers essential to his or her identity. In fact, some might consider it insulting to lump everyone's beliefs together, which is in fact equivalent to ignoring their beliefs, for the sake of diversity. The culturally competent health care practitioner goes out of his or her way to learn intimate details about the different worldviews that his or her patients might hold onto as part of their identity.

Understanding different worldviews is critically important to culturally competent health care. Interestingly, worldviews are often unknown or ignored by many health care practitioners. However, worldviews are the foundation of diversity and cultural competency and have a profound impact on a person's values and beliefs about health care. In fact, some would argue that it is impossible to practice evidence-based practice correctly without a firm understanding of worldviews. That argument is based on the fact that one of the 3 aspects of evidence-based practice (EMP) is patient expectations/values. In fact, Sackett et al[2] state EBP includes, "compassionate use of individual patients' preferences." Therefore, it is incumbent upon any health care provider to understand worldviews, so that he or she knows what influences his or her patient's expectations.

An individual's worldview is a set of conscious and subconscious presuppositions about the basic makeup of the world.[3] Some people use the term paradigm as a substitute for worldview. Worldview represents the ideas and beliefs through which an individual interprets the reality of the world around him or her. As stated in the definition, sometimes the basis of this interpretation is obvious or known to the individual and other times it is subconscious or out of his or her conscious awareness. Regardless, it has a profound impact on how he or she receives care and expresses his or her appreciation for that care. And for us in the Western world, that has a direct outcome on patient satisfaction scores and other patient outcomes. It is necessary that we know what the different worldviews are.

Every single person has a worldview whether they are aware of it or not, and scholars recommended 7 basic questions that can serve as a way to discover one's worldview.[3] Those 7 questions are:

1. **What is real (or what do you consider ultimate reality)?**—This answer determines the source one seeks for reassurance and help when injured or ill.

2. **What is the nature of reality?**—This answer helps to explain the existence or reason patients may believe they are sick or injured.

3. **What is a human being?**—This answer may determine the amount of value or worth an individual places on a human life.

4. **What happens to a person after death?**—This answer determines the level of hope for peace a person can experience when sick or injured.

5. **Is it possible to know anything?**—This answer determines the value of evidence and research used in treatment.

6. **How do we know what is right and wrong?**—This answer gets to the heart of medical ethics and a clinician's behavior and attitude towards patients.

7. **What is the meaning or purpose of human history?**—This answer provides insight into the patient's perception of purpose and destiny and may serve to rationalize sickness or injury.

These may appear on the surface to be extremely philosophical questions, and indeed they may be, but they form every person's ideology. According to Sire[3], there are 8 dominant worldviews. Sire[3] believes that every human being has a worldview (or mix of worldviews) that address the 7 questions listed previously. The 8 worldviews are:

1. **Theism:** Theism can be divided into monotheism and polytheism. What many people consider to be the 3 great or foundational religions of the world are monotheistic and include Christianity, Judaism, and Islam. These 3 major world religions are theistic and hold the belief that there is one personal God. Polytheism is a belief that there are many gods responsible for the human condition. An example of polytheism would be Hinduism.

   a. Take a moment to consider the diversity within Theism alone. In response to the 7 questions above, each one of the 4 world religions mentioned (Christianity, Judaism, Islam, and Hinduism) would answer the 7 questions differently. Not being aware of how a

Christian vs a Hindu might answer the questions can dramatically impact the care they are given and receive. Some could argue that not being alert to that could be considered negligent.

2. **Deism:** Deism is closely tied to monotheism and believes that there is a God, or at least a divine creator, but that the creator does not intervene with what was created. The foundational tenet of this worldview is that God does exist, but does not care and is watching from a distance.

3. **Naturalism:** Naturalism is a belief in the scientific method. Its basic supposition is that observation and reason are the sole criteria for truth and anything that cannot be observed or explained is not real.

4. **Nihilism:** Nihilism is the belief that it is not possible to know anything, that nothing in-and-of itself has any inherent value, and that everything a person experiences or suffers in life is meaningless.

5. **Existentialism:** Existentialism is the belief that humanity is the only significant expression in the world. That the essence of a person comes before his or her existence. Truth can only be discovered by seeking something or someone's true essence.

6. **Pantheism:** Pantheism is the belief that everything is connected to the divine and that the divine can be seen anywhere in anything. Pantheists hold the view that everything (even sentient and nonsentient beings) has equal value. For example, animals, humans, and plants all have equal value and worth because the essence of life or God is in everything.

7. **New Ageism:** New Ageism is a worldview for people who cannot decide their worldview. It is an eclectic mix of several worldviews to suit the whims of individuals who do not care for critical self-reflection.

8. **Postmodernism:** Postmodernism is not a true worldview per se, but it is a framework based on a value system that many people hold. Postmodernists believe that all knowledge is valuable and equal, wrong or good and bad are in the eye of the beholder, and that what is right for one person may be wrong for another or vice versa, and therefore, everyone's truth is acceptable. Which by implication means there is nothing ever that can be wrong or proven otherwise.

These are the 8 basic worldviews of the world. Most people do not intentionally think of themselves as Deists, Nihilists, or Postmodernists, per se; it is important to ask and answer the 7 questions because in answering those 7 questions you can determine which worldview you are most likely to hold to. This discussion has tremendous value when discussing cultural competency, diversity, and patient's values and expectations. Without a keen awareness of the different worldviews and the profound impact it has on how a patient receives care and how a practitioner practices care, we will never truly be culturally competent. Introducing the concept of worldviews means that dialogue about diversity, globalization, and cultural competency should never be about accepting everyone beliefs and values as correct—by definition that would undermine the purpose of diversity in the first place—but they should be about understanding and appreciating the values and expectations of others.

Discussion Questions

1. Based on the abbreviated descriptions provided in this chapter, what is your dominant worldview?

2. How would you expect conflict in your worldview and your patient's worldview to play out in a clinical scenario? (For example, your patient believes there is a God who is involved and has a purpose, but you do not ... your patient is a Theist and you are a Deist).

3. What are some things that you can engage in to help you learn about the nuances of different worldviews?

4. How might knowing the different worldviews that could be possibly held by your patients impact how you lead your department?

5. What are some policies and procedures for which you might advocate or implement within your organization to better facilitate cultural competency through an understanding of different worldviews?

References

1. Kutz MR. *Leadership and Management in Athletic Training: An Integrated Approach*. Philadelphia, PA: Lippincott Williams & Wilkins; 2010.

2. Sackett DL, Rosenberg WM, Gray JA, Haynes RB, Richardson WS. Evidence based medicine: what it is and what it isn't. *BMJ*. 1996;312(7023):71-72.

3. Sire JW. *The Universe Next Door: A Basic Worldview Catalog*. Downers Grove, IL: InterVarsity Press; 2009.

Index